Finding Eternal Life

A Forty Day Spiritual Encounter

by

Dennis Kaufman

First published by AuthorHouse 06/07/04

ISBN: 1-4184-6394-9 (e-book)
ISBN: 1-4184-3526-0 (Paperback)

Library of Congress Control Number: 2004092125

This book is printed on acid free paper.

Printed in the United States of America
Bloomington, IN

ILLUSTRATION by Andrea N. Gaines

Cover illustration by Christina N. Kaufman

Table of Contents

WHY FORTY DAYS

(Note: Boldface emphasis is mine.)

"I will send rain on the earth for **forty days** and **forty nights** . . ." (Genesis 7:4).

"When Moses went up on the mountain, the cloud covered it, and the glory of the LORD settled on Mount Sinai. For six days the cloud covered the mountain, and on the seventh day the LORD called to Moses from within the cloud. To the Israelites the glory of the LORD looked like a consuming fire on top of the mountain. Then Moses entered the cloud as he went on up the mountain. And he stayed on the mountain **forty days** and **forty nights**" (Exodus 24:15-18).

"I [Moses] lay prostrate before the Lord those **forty days** and **forty nights** . . ." (Deuteronomy 9:25).

"So he [Elijah] got up and ate and drank. Strengthened by that food, he traveled **forty days** and **forty nights** until he reached Horeb, the mountain of God" 1 (Kings 19:8).

"Jesus, full of the Holy Spirit, returned from the Jordan and was led by the Spirit in the desert, where for **forty days** he was tempted by the devil . . ." (Luke 4:1,2).

"After his suffering [and resurrection] he showed himself to these men and gave many convincing proofs that he was alive. He appeared to them over a period of **forty days** and spoke about the kingdom of God" (Acts 1:3).

The Bible records that only Jesus, Moses, and Elijah fasted forty days. (Please don't think I'm suggesting that you should fast during the reading of this book!) That noted, and as suggested by the Scripture above, forty represents a period set apart for consecration to a cause. Thus, for the next forty days, as you begin and end your day with a devotional, you will be on a mission.

Yet, the forty-day format is a tool, not a necessity. The journey to Eternal Life can take forty days, one day, or a lifetime. Thankfully, the timetable is in God's hands.

WHY YOU NEED THIS BOOK

You're fortunate to discover this book, though you may be sorry now that you bought it— or that someone gave it to you— or that the book came to you unexpectedly. You may be tempted to toss it, yet you're curiously drawn to its contents.

Why? Because you've tried everything else and you haven't found peace. What do you fear? Death? Poverty? Divorce? Mental illness? Losing control? Sickness? Pain? Abuse? Addiction? Loneliness? Losing your job? God can help you overcome these fears, even if He is your only and last hope. Don't look inside yourself. The answer's not there. Trust in the unseen, outside you and infinitely greater than you. Then expect to be rewarded for your faith. ". . . Blessed are those who have not seen and yet have believed" (John 20:29).

What you're holding in your hands, this journey of faith, may lead you to One who has been the last resort for many. Hebrews 11:1 says, "Now faith is being sure of what we hope for and certain of what we do not see." Yet for honest seekers of faith, for Gentiles and for Jews, this encounter won't be another dead end.

As in geometry, where you define a point before a line and a line before a polygon, there's a logical path to help you find the way to God. Follow the daily readings in sequence. Each step builds faith for the next encounter. Your faith grows as you conquer each idea and the idea conquers you.

If you can, make time to find the verses in your own Bible and then try reading them aloud. Doing so gives authority to God's Word. (Note: Most readings are from the New International Version; KJV indicates the passage is from the King James Version.)

Lastly, say the prayers silently or aloud even if that's awkward at first. Use your own prayers to God if you can. There's no magic in the sample prayers. They're here to guide you into natural speech with your Creator.

During the journey, I hope you'll experience a revelation. You'll say the Name and heaven will open to you. The event happens in as many ways as there are individuals. When heaven responds, you can then begin a new pilgrimage, the journey of living in Eternal Life.

"Seek— you'll find. Knock— the door will open." It's now opened a crack. Your sincere effort to enter is noticed. Soon a light will go on in the darkened room beyond. Not only do you find God, but also He finds you! Come out of the wilderness. Find Eternal Life!

PRAYER: *"Dear God, I ask for this reader to come to know You in a special way, personal to them and ordained by You. That the faith You give to them will bring them to Eternal Life. Please overcome the inadequacy of these words, and let Your revelation be with the power of divine speech and in signs that You deem appropriate. Illuminate this book, in clarity, relevance, and truth by the light of Your Holy Spirit. I ask that You make Yourself known to the reader. I pray in the Name above all names, Amen."*

DAY 01 — DAYBREAK The Evidence In Creation.

READING

". . . What may be known about God is plain to them, because God has made it plain to them. For since the creation of the world God's invisible qualities— His eternal power and divine nature— have been clearly seen, being understood from what has been made, so that men are without excuse" (Romans 1:19, 20).

ENCOUNTER

If a tree falls in the forest with no human witnesses, has it fallen? Ah, but Someone does see this event: He who created the trees and the earth itself. Psalm 65:6, 7 says, ". . . Who formed the mountains by your power, having armed yourself with strength, who stilled the roaring of the seas . . .". In the New Testament we read, ". . . The living God, who made heaven and earth and sea and everything in them" (Acts 14:15).

God is real! God exists! His full glory is veiled, yet we sense the existence of a greater power. And He knows our every thought. In a crisis or in death's grip we cry out, "Please, God, don't let me die. Not yet." In our hearts, we know He's real. We only have to be warmed by the sunshine or carried along by a mighty wind to feel His touch.

He shows His existence in minutiae— molecules, cells, subatomic particles, nuclei, and electrons—and in the macrocosm. Vast untracked space, the constellations, Saturn, Jupiter, Alpha Centauri, and black holes all point to God as Creator.

Psalm 104:6 says, "He set the earth on its foundations . . .". And we read in Acts 14:17, "Yet he has not left himself without testimony . . . giving you rain from heaven and crops in their seasons." He's as certain as the four seasons! Job writes, "He alone stretches out the heavens and treads on the waves of the sea. He is the Maker of the Bear and Orion, the Pleiades and the constellations of the south" (Job 9:8, 9). The Big Dipper reveals God's sense of humor.

Though "you know that you know" God exists, yet you rebel and deny the truth. We have a built-in assurance, even a comfort, that God is real. In Psalm 14:1 we read, "The fool says in his heart, 'There is no God.'" Yet, I'm responsible for my destiny and carry my mortality like a ticking time bomb.

You can develop systems of knowledge, but you can't deny Truth. You cannot disprove God's existence. And why should you? God gave the world life and He's our only hope for Eternal Life. Know that you can't ignore God forever. In fact, someday you'll meet Him. A genuine seeker will find God because He exists. And God is patient.

". . . Turn from these worthless things to the living God, who made heaven and earth and sea and everything in them" (Acts 14:15).

PRAY: *"Almighty Creator, when I see the glorious creation, life and death, let me see You. Reveal a glimpse of Your majesty to me."*

DAY 01 — SUNDOWN The Evidence in the Writings.

READING

". . . From infancy you have known the holy Scriptures, which are able to make you wise for salvation through faith in Christ Jesus. All Scripture is God-breathed" (2 Timothy 3:15).

ENCOUNTER

God told Abram, "I am God Almighty. . . " (Genesis 17:1). What book dares to quote God speaking in the first person to a man? What other book has the audacity to describe the origin of the universe in the first sentence? Remember Genesis 1:1, "In the beginning God created . . ."

God still speaks today. He's taken the initiative to reveal Himself. The Bible is God's complete, unchanging Word for man. The Bible is His voice, where God unveils Himself in the longest letter ever written. The Bible arouses in us a sense of God's regal independence, absolute authority, and epic character. We only truly appreciate the writings once we fall in love with God.

The Scriptures are holy because God is holy. We're created knowing right and wrong, but on the journey, life hardens us so we compromise or abandon those principles. This sacred writing can bring us back. Just as we see God in creation, we know the Bible is divinely inspired. Reading God's Word puts faith and wisdom in our hearts and minds and leads to salvation.

People of many faiths recognize the authority of the Bible and accept most portions of the Bible as holy truth. The Bible dares to prophesy the knowledge of the future, and the predictions within its covers have all come true . . . perfectly. Perfect foreknowledge can only come from God.

Jesus says in Luke 21:33, "Heaven and earth will pass away, but my words will never pass away." Then He goes on to validate the entire Old Covenant in Luke 24:44, "Everything must be fulfilled that is written about me in the Law of Moses, the Prophets and the Psalms." In John 21:25 the disciple John says that if all said and done by Jesus were recorded, "The whole world would not have room for the books that would be written." Just enough is written to bring us to know God.

The Roman governor Pontius Pilate asked Jesus the day He died, "What is truth?" (John 18:38) That question is still foremost today. Jesus' answer reads, ". . . I came into the world, to testify to the truth. Everyone on the side of truth listens to me" (John 18:37).

Jesus says, "You diligently study the Scriptures because you think that by them you possess eternal life. These are the Scriptures that testify about me, yet you refuse to come to me to have life" (John 5:39, 40). Welcome the Bible like a lifesaver— come to the truth and be saved. ". . . Know the truth, and the truth will set you free" (John 8:32). We <u>can</u> know the truth, though now we only hear it as a bell ringing faintly in a distant room.

On every page the personality, the mind, the motives, the thoughts, the purpose, and the will of God speak to the needs of the reader. As a guide for human behavior, the Bible is relevant to men and women in all ages and of all ages. Other books I read, but the Bible is the only book that reads me. It speaks to my mind. It sings my song to my heart.

PRAY: *"Lord, please help me understand Your Word, the Bible. Lead me to the pages with a personal message for me."*

DAY 02 — DAYBREAK The Revelation.

READING

". . . No prophecy of Scripture came about by the prophet's own interpretation. For prophecy never had its origin in the will of man, but men spoke from God . . . by the Holy Spirit" (2 Peter 1:20, 21).

ENCOUNTER

Over forty different men, of vastly different origins, independently inspired by God for over fifteen hundred years, wrote sixty-six unique, yet elaborate, and interconnected books that became known as the Bible. Scholars estimate that men wrote the Bible between 1400 B.C. and A.D. 90. No other ancient literature comes close to the number of biblical manuscripts found. Although it's almost impossible to comprehend how, the books are unified into one symphony because they share the same source. ". . . The word of God, which you heard from us, you accepted it not as the word of men, but as . . . the word of God . . ." (1 Thessalonians 2:13).

Is the Bible a collection of myths? Discoveries by astronomers and archaeologists only strengthen biblical facts. For example, it's now widely believed the flood that Noah experienced occurred. Most early civilizations tell of a flood and an ark in their mythology. And the Grand Canyon couldn't be carved by the Colorado River alone!

Also, a true Old Covenant prophet was above reproach. If he lied or was wrong, he was stoned! "But a prophet who presumes to speak in my name anything I have not commanded him to say, or a prophet who speaks in the name of other gods, must be put to death" (Deuteronomy 18:20). Micaiah, a prophet of integrity said, "As surely as the LORD lives, I can tell him only what the LORD tells me" (1 Kings 22:14). The character of the New Testament writers is evidence that the writings were not fabricated. At times they show themselves in a bad light . . . James and John sought high positions in Messiah's new political order, the lack of courage shown by the disciples when the Romans captured Jesus, Jesus' own fears at Gethsemane, and so on. Then there are extrabiblical writings from the first century that validate the writers of the New Testament.

The way the Bible was preserved also lends credence to its contents. God chose the Jewish race to preserve His written Word for centuries. Scribes meticulously copied millions of characters by hand onto leather and parchment. The monastic Essenes secreted an entire library to the Qumran caves by the Dead Sea. The complete Isaiah scroll and segments from every Bible book, all over two thousand years old, were found in 1948 with other Essene writings. The Dead Sea Bible portions, the oldest existing manuscript today, are identical with the modern versions. Hardly a word was lost or changed in two thousand years. The Dead Sea Scrolls show the original inspiration is preserved and is divinely protected. "The grass withers and the flowers fall, but the word of our God stands forever" (Isaiah 40:8).

A limestone ossuary (bone box), dating to the first century, was found in Israel with the Aramaic inscription, "James, son of Joseph, the brother of Jesus." Some experts believe the box to be the one that once held the remains of James, Jesus' half-brother. Of course, Joseph, James's father, was the husband of Mary. Rarely are burial boxes found inscribed with the name of a sibling—unless he was Jesus Christ. Yes, science continues to validate the truth of the Bible.

PRAY: *"Dear God, show me how the Bible is a map of the only road urgently needing to be traveled. Make it relevant to me so that it speaks to me."*

DAY 02 — SUNDOWN The Revelation.

READING

"That which was from the beginning, which we have heard, which we have seen with our eyes, which we have looked at and our hands have touched— this we proclaim concerning the Word of life. The life appeared; we have seen it and testify to it, and we proclaim to you the eternal life, which was with the Father and has appeared to us . . ." (1 John 1:1-3).

"We did not follow cleverly invented stories when we told you about the power and coming of our Lord Jesus Christ, but we were eyewitnesses of his majesty" (2 Peter 1:16).

"Men of Israel, listen to this: Jesus of Nazareth was a man accredited by God to you by miracles, wonders and signs, which God did among you through him, as you yourselves know" (Acts 2:22).

" . . . These are written, that you might believe that Jesus is the Christ, the Son of God; and that by believing you may have life in his name" (John 20:31).

ENCOUNTER

The Bible presents the evidence of Matthew, Mark, John, Peter, Luke, and other eyewitnesses of the promised Messiah. You might expect biblical accounts by multiple writers to be inconsistent and contradictory. Yet the opposite is true. The Bible is completely unified and without error. That there are differences in the Gospels, without contradiction, only lends an aspect of truth.

Luke 2:26 speaks of a devout man Simeon: "It had been revealed to him by the Holy Spirit that he would not die before he had seen the Lord's Christ." In 2003, Simeon's sixty-foot tomb was found in Kidron Valley in Jerusalem. The words of Luke 2:25 are carved on it in Greek, "Now there was a man in Jerusalem called Simeon, who was righteous and devout. He was waiting for the consolation of Israel." Even the obscure people in the Bible existed; the accounts are true.

Old Covenant writings became alive through revelation in the person of God's living Son. John 1:14 says, "The Word became flesh and made his dwelling among us. We have seen his glory, the glory of the One and Only, who came from the Father . . .".

The revelation is on the printed page or spoken word, bearing witness to God's existence, declaring we may learn the mystery of eternity. Indeed, God's Word transforms us. Reading and hearing, we begin to believe in the Son of God. As we believe in His Son, God approaches us. He gives us inner peace for daily living and for eternal assurance.

Though we fear death, if we secure Eternal Life before we die, we can pass from this life to the hereafter in peace and in safety. When you attain Eternal Life, you're certain of it. Christians have hope and faith to cross "the valley of the shadow of death" in confidence.

John 5:24 says, "I tell you the truth, whoever hears my [Jesus'] word and believes him who sent me has eternal life and will not be condemned; he has crossed over from death to life." We also read, "In him was life, and that life was the light of men. The light shines in the darkness, but the darkness has not understood it" (John 1:4, 5). The revelation is a person, Jesus Christ.

PRAY: *"Help me to understand the mystery of eternity. Reveal Your Son to me."*

DAY 03 — DAYBREAK Preexistence.

READING

"Before the mountains were born or you brought forth the earth and the world, from everlasting to everlasting you are God" (Psalm 90:2).

"By faith we understand that the universe was formed at God's command, so that what is seen was not made out of what was visible" (Hebrews 11:3).

ENCOUNTER

Before the vacuum of space, before relentless time and celestial objects, before life, before death, a Being existed who is the "uncaused cause." Before the universe was born, God, whom we cannot see in our mortal state, lived in glorious light that penetrated the blackness. God spoke and the physical universe was created during the six Ages (Days).

Age 1: Light in the void.

Age 2: Heaven.

Age 3: Earth and vegetation.

Age 4: Heavenly bodies and the seasons.

Age 5: Creatures of sea and air.

Age 6: Creatures of land, then Man in God's image.

Age 7: God rests.

It's unlikely each "Day" was twenty-four hours since the sun wasn't created until the fourth Day. *Yom*, the Hebrew word for Day, also means a long time, a season, or a whole period. Whether each Age was literally one solar day or hundreds of thousands of years, God could easily create with the appearance of aging.

"Can God build a wall He can't climb?" The question avoids the real point: Does God exist? If God wants to limit His own free will, He can. Would God allow His Son to be killed without intervening? The answer is the same.

Lord Kelvin's Second Law of Thermodynamics states, "The extent of disorder, or entropy, in the universe can only increase." This law contradicts evolution because over time there should be chaos, not order. God oversees everything. Without Him there would be disorder; the universe would be unstructured and confusion would reign. God is from before time. Unhindered by limits, He knows and foreknows. God personifies Infinity.

He is the First and the Last – from A to Z – *Alpha* to *Omega* – *Aleph* to *Tawv*

He is the Beginning and the End – from Infinity to Infinity – Everlasting to Everlasting

In the scheme of everlasting, the plodding earth in its orbit is like a slowly spinning top on a child's table. The concept of infinity dwarfs our life, with its starting point and fixed duration. Yet the stage of our limited mortality is the arena in which we must search to find Eternal Life.

PRAY: *"What riches in You. I want to know You!*

DAY 03 — SUNDOWN Preexistence.

READING

". . . He who made you, who formed you in the womb, and who will help you . . ." (Isaiah 44:2).

"For you created my inmost being; you knit me together in my mother's womb. I praise you because I am fearfully and wonderfully made; your works are wonderful, I know that full well. My frame was not hidden from you when I was made in the secret place. When I was woven together in the depths of the earth, your eyes saw my unformed body. All the days ordained for me were written in your book before one of them came to be" (Psalm 139:13-16).

"Yet you brought me out of the womb; you made me trust in you even at my mother's breast. From birth I was cast upon you; from my mother's womb you have been my God" (Psalm 22:9, 10).

ENCOUNTER

As written in Genesis 1, all life was made "according to its kind," animals after animals, plants after plants. Animals don't come from plants. People don't come from animals. Human life is sanctified because man is made in God's image. God loved us before our birth, before the universe was born, when we were an element of His mind. He was pleased to create us. His desire was for us to be. We're given a place in history.

Though humans have creative intellect, which is a gift from God as our Creator, God was not obliged to give us perfect free will. We're not able to know the time or the method of our death. God doesn't ask our souls before we're conceived if we want to live. Romans 9:20, 21 says, ". . . Who are you, O man, to talk back to God? Shall what is formed say to him who formed it, 'Why did you make me like this?' Does not the potter have the right to make out of the same lump of clay some pottery for noble purposes and some for common use?"

The moment of life, when the egg and seed of our parents unite, is our conception. When the two cells unite they form a whole greater than the original parts. Your soul is sealed into the zygote. The seal makes the moment of procreation a spiritual and a physical event, a moment when God's miracle explodes into creation.

Jesus even prayed for you before you were born. In this, His "High Priestly Prayer," Jesus asked His Father to give you eternal life. ". . . You granted him [Jesus] authority over all people that he might give eternal life to all those you have given him. Now this is eternal life: that they may know you, the only true God, and Jesus Christ, whom you have sent. I have brought you glory on earth by completing the work you gave me to do. And now, Father, glorify me in your presence with the glory I had with you before the world began. I have revealed you to those whom you gave me out of the world. They were yours; you gave them to me and they have obeyed your word. My prayer is not for them alone. I pray also for those who will believe in me through their message" (John 17:2-6, 20).

We're important to God. Rejoice that you were given life and a unique personality. Lament for those that could have been created but were not, those who might have been but are not.

PRAY: *"Thank You."*

DAY 04 — DAYBREAK The Beginning.

READING

"In the beginning God created the heavens and the earth. Now the earth was formless and empty, darkness was over the surface of the deep, and the Spirit of God was hovering over the waters. And God said, 'Let there be light,' and there was light . . ." (Genesis 1:1-3).

"For by him all things were created: things in heaven and on earth, visible and invisible . . ." (Colossians 1:16).

"By faith we understand that the universe was formed at God's command, so that what is seen was not made out of what was visible" (Hebrews 11:3).

ENCOUNTER

There was a beginning, a first event. Physicists generally agree that a cataclysmic eruption or "Big Bang" birthed the universe. Space and time began, *ex nihilo*, from nothing. Massively dense hydrogen, the simplest element, fueled the reaction as a fireball of searing light and heat burst outward, creating the cosmos. As matter cooled, stars formed at compressed points in hydrogen clouds. In an ether of stellar matter and energy, elements that are more complex and the planets formed.

The Hebrew words for waters, *Mayim* (Genesis 1:3), and for heavens, *Shamayim* (Genesis 1:6), are similar. Because water is composed of two parts hydrogen, I propose the writer of Genesis used the term "water" to try to explain hydrogen.

Scientists can observe the galaxies moving apart from the earth, and apart from each other, at incredible speed as the universe rushes outward and away from the original explosion. Further, scientists measure background heat radiation that drifts to earth from space, the remains of the creation moment, a witness to the birth of the universe.

Clearly, the biblical account and the scientific account are in harmony. Scientists derive conclusions from physical evidence that support the Genesis narrative. Astronomers and theologians agree the universe had a beginning. But was it formed naturally or supernaturally?

Where did the energy come from that converted to matter to resolve the equation $E = mc^2$? Why is there a universe? What's the probability that life began by accident? Experts can't answer who created the physical laws, but the Bible does: In prehistory, God willed the universe into place.

The dilemmas created by unbelief in God exceed those of faith. "For the scientist who has lived by his faith in the power of reason, the story ends like a bad dream. He has scaled the mountains of ignorance; he is about to conquer the highest peak; as he pulls himself over the final rock, he is greeted by a band of theologians who have been sitting there for centuries." [1]

PRAY: *"The universe is vast. It's hard to imagine what Person caused it. Show me . . . if You exist!"*

DAY 04 — SUNDOWN The Beginning.

READING

"Then God said, 'Let us make man in our image, in our likeness, and let them rule over the fish of the sea and the birds of the air, over the livestock, over all the earth, and over all the creatures that move along the ground.' So God created man in his own image, in the image of God he created him; male and female he created them" (Genesis 1:26, 27).

ENCOUNTER

Science claims that primitive cells formed from nonliving matter. Evolution theory needs countless years to pass for the advancement to complex life and then, "hello man." An enormous passage of time, a necessity for evolution, also causes problems for the theory.

For example, the oceans should be much saltier than they are. If man has procreated since evolutionists say, we should already be standing shoulder to shoulder and piled up from overpopulation! Why haven't extreme forms of mutancy evolved, like horse-dogs, ape-men, three-eyed and four-armed men, and people with faces in front and back? Where are the dinosaurs? They definitely existed, but they must have disappeared in the Flood or had some other lethal fate.

Science, like some religions, also can embrace myths. Evolution is theory, not fact! Experts dismiss once accepted theories, like linking ape to man through Piltdown and Cro-Magnon man. The world of science questions the basics of evolution, but those doubts don't reach the popular thinking. Dead scientific theories live on as public mythology.

"Scientists have dealt a blow to the idea that modern humans arose simultaneously in different parts of the world. Analyzing a gene on the Y chromosome of thirty-eight men from all over the globe, they found no variation – and thus concluded that humanity's ancestors formed a small, concentrated population as recently as 270,000 years ago. Earlier studies reached the same conclusion by looking at a different sort of genetic material in women." [2] The discoveries affirm that humans descended through one family, first through Adam, and then through Noah.

Who was the first mother? If male and female evolved independently, why is their sexual union needed to produce a child in the highly coordinated mating process? And children should be born from either partner!

Where's the evidence in the soil to conclude mammals came from reptiles that crawled out of the oceans? The variety of animals of similar look and structure can point to the same designer, the same Creator. The laboratory reproduces the conditions for life but it hasn't produced <u>life</u> there. Science has no explanation for the beginning. Faith is required to believe in either natural evolution or miraculous creation.

Because God created man in His image, we're valuable. We're special. We're unique. Humanity is a family of sons and daughters, brothers and sisters, linked by God. Evolution deceives men and women into accepting a kingdom of self-preservation, without genuine interest in brotherhood.

PRAY: *"I want to see Your print on creation, that the possibility of God will be, in my mind, in line with scientific evidence."*

DAY 05 — DAYBREAK The Tri-Unity.

READING

"Come near me and listen to this: 'From the first announcement I have not spoken in secret; at the time it happens, I am there.' And now the Sovereign LORD has sent me, with his Spirit" (Isaiah 48:16, 17).

ENCOUNTER

"God is life." "God is all people." "God is everything." "God is in me." Naturalism says that only the physical (experienced with the five senses) is reality, that God doesn't exist, or if He does, we can't know it. Is it honest to design a personal god, predetermine a list of attributes, and then expect God will fit the conditions?

The Bible says that there is a plurality in the Godhead, i.e., one God of three personalities or three distinct Persons. There is a Father, a Son, and a Holy Spirit. Deuteronomy 6:4 says, "Hear, Oh Israel: The LORD [*Yahweh*] Our God [*Elohanu*], The LORD [*Yahweh*] is one [*Echad*]" (emphasis mine).

Stanley Rosenthal has called the Trinity the Tri-Unity. Isaiah 48:16 refers to the Tri-Unity, and the word "me" refers to the Son or Messiah, "And now the Sovereign LORD has sent me, with his Spirit." *Echad* is translated as a unity of one, a composite of one, a plurality of one. *Echad* is used in other biblical verses to explain the "first day" as Night and Day, "one flesh" for husband and wife, and "one cluster" of grapes. Note further that one of God's names in Hebrew, *Elohim*, is a plural word. *Elohim* is used 2500 times versus the singular form of God, *El,* used only 250 times. [3]

Moses asked God, ". . . Suppose I go to the Israelites and say to them, 'The God of your fathers has sent me to you,' and they ask me, 'What is his name?' Then what shall I tell them?" God repeats His name three times in response: ". . . I AM WHO I AM. This is what you are to say to the Israelites: 'I AM has sent me to you'" (Exodus 3:13, 14, emphasis mine). *Yahweh, Yahweh, Yahweh*!

The angels sing around His throne in Revelation 4:8 and Isaiah 6:3: "Holy, holy, holy is the LORD Almighty" (emphasis mine). They repeat the word "Holy" for each person of God.

God repeats His name three times in Zechariah. ". . . Lo, I come, and I will dwell in the midst of thee, saith the Lord Jehovah. And many nations shall be joined to the Lord Jehovah, in that day, and shall be my people: and I will dwell in the midst of thee, and thou shalt know that the Lord Jehovah of hosts hath sent me unto thee" (Zechariah 2:10, 11, KJV, emphasis mine).

The Lord said He would come to dwell among men. Then Jesus Christ came in the person of an infant who is also the Father. "For unto us a child is born, to us a son is given, and the government will be on his shoulders. And he will be called Wonderful Counselor, Mighty God, Everlasting Father, Prince of Peace" (Isaiah 9:6, 7).

One can talk about the Tri-Unity, but the concept is barely understandable. I'll grasp it when I see Him face to face.

PRAY: *"Awesome God, reach out to me at a place I understand."*

DAY 05 — SUNDOWN The Tri-Unity.

READING

"As soon as Jesus was baptized, he went up out of the water. At that moment heaven was opened, and he saw the Spirit of God descending like a dove and lighting on him. And a voice from heaven said, 'This is my Son, whom I love; with him I am well pleased'" (Matthew 3:16, 17).

ENCOUNTER

Jesus stood in the gently moving Jordan River. The Nazarite prophet, John the Baptist, wearing rugged camelhair clothes, immersed his cousin (on his mother's side) beneath the waters. As Jesus emerged, God the Father, from heaven, endorsed Jesus as His Son. The Father sent the Holy Spirit, symbolized by the dove. The scene displays the three persons of the Tri-Unity.

God reveals He has three facets of His character. The three Persons of His complex nature are not evidence of paganism or multiple gods. Polytheism is the worship of independent "gods" that are in no way related. The Tri-Unity is the mystifying divinity of one perfectly unified God. In fact, God refers to Himself in the plural in the first chapter of the Bible. "Then God said, 'Let <u>us</u> make man in <u>our</u> image, in <u>our</u> likeness . . .'" (Genesis 1:26, emphasis mine).

Isaiah 61:1, a Messianic reference says, "The Spirit of the Sovereign LORD is on me, because the LORD has anointed me to preach good news to the poor. He has sent me to bind up the brokenhearted, to proclaim freedom for the captives and release from darkness for the prisoners." In the Nazareth synagogue, Jesus interpreted this verse, proclaiming that the "me" mentioned by Isaiah was Himself (Luke 4:18). After reading the Isaiah scroll Jesus said, "Today this scripture is fulfilled in your hearing" (Luke 4:20).

In the New Testament, in Hebrews 1:2, 3, we read, "But in these last days he has spoken to us by his Son, whom he appointed heir of all things, and through whom he made the universe. The Son is the radiance of God's glory and the exact representation of his being . . .". God created the universe by His Son Jesus, who was there at the start. Since Genesis says, "God created," logically, Jesus is God.

"Who has gone up to heaven and come down? Who has gathered up the wind in the hollow of his hands? Who has wrapped up the waters in his cloak? Who has established all the ends of the earth? What is his name, and the name of his son? Tell me if you know!" (Proverbs 30:4). The ancient question is answered in the Father and in the Son. God has a Son!

As early as the first chapter of the Bible, God says His Spirit, is a manifestation of the Father. ". . . And the Spirit of God was hovering over the waters" (Genesis 1:2).

Jesus said, ". . . I am in my Father, and you are in me, and I am in you" (John 14:20). Jesus also said, "I came from the Father and entered the world; now I am leaving the world and going back to the Father" (John 16:28).

The mystery of the Tri-Unity really can't be explained. God is complex, yet elegant. He is Three in One. One! "The Lord our God, the Lord is One!" (Deuteronomy 6:4).

PRAY: *"Help me not just to try to understand, but to believe."*

DAY 06 — DAYBREAK Predestiny.

READING

". . . He chose us in him before the creation of the world to be holy and blameless in his sight. In love he predestined us to be adopted as his sons through Jesus Christ, in accordance with his pleasure and will" (Ephesians 1:4, 5).

"In him [Christ] we were also chosen, having been predestined according to the plan of him who works out everything in conformity with the purpose of his will" (Ephesians 1:11).

ENCOUNTER

In the Book of Genesis, we read that Joseph's half-brothers envied him because he was the favorite son of their father Jacob. The conflict became a crisis after Joseph told them his dream, that he would rule them. For that, His brothers sold him to slave traders en route to Egypt. Joseph's destiny, to become Pharaoh's co-ruler in Egypt, was a crucible of fiery trials. God's purpose unfolded just as Joseph's dream foretold.

Joseph's family fled to Egypt from a famine in Israel. There they reunited with Joseph who had become royalty. A spiritually sensitive man, Joseph realized that God engineered his reversals. Instead of taking revenge on his brothers, Joseph announced, in Genesis 45:5, ". . . Do not be distressed and do not be angry with yourselves for selling me here, because it was to save lives that God sent me ahead of you." Joseph learned how God predestined his life.

In Acts 9:15 we read that God ordained the apostle Paul saying, ". . . This man is my chosen instrument to carry my name. . .". All people are born in God's image, but only some born in God's image are adopted into His family as children of God. God predestines only some as sons and daughters. John 15:16 says, "You did not choose me, but I chose you . . ." and John 15:19 reads, ". . . I have chosen you out of the world . . .".

You say, "But I don't want to believe in a God who allows some to go to heaven and not all!" God provides for all to go heaven but He knows some won't accept His offer of salvation. You counter, "Doesn't predestiny limit my freedom to live?" Providence reduces the field of choices but not my freedom to choose. God gave me restricted free will. We have no choice but to trust in God's objectivity and His perfect justice.

Is there then a plan you should follow? Predestiny is God's foreknowledge, but it shouldn't immobilize us. We aren't slaves or robots. I must act upon whatever free will I was given. My mind may not allow me to dwell on death, but **I know I'm going to die** physically! There's freedom before we die, but obviously no amount of free will allows us to escape death.

"For many are invited, but few are chosen" (Matthew 22:14). God invites you to throw yourself on His goodness. Some people are chosen, but few will give up, acknowledge their weakness, and receive the invitation to God's forgiveness. God's favored family thanks Him in gratitude, realizing the depth of love He has for all people.

PRAY: *"God, please help me understand and accept the reality of predestiny and limited free will with impartiality."*

DAY 06 — SUNDOWN Predestiny.

READING

". . . He is patient with you, not wanting anyone to perish, but everyone to come to repentance" (2 Peter 3:9).

"Woe to him who quarrels with his Maker . . . Does the clay say to the potter, 'What are you making?'" (Isaiah 45:9).

"Who have been chosen according to the foreknowledge of God the Father . . ." (1 Peter 1:2).

ENCOUNTER

We're each born on a sinking ship—and there are the lifeboats lowered below the listing deck with some empty seats. The question begs to be asked: Why do some choose God when He reaches out while others reject Him?

". . . Children being not yet born, neither having done any good or evil, that the purpose of God according to election might stand, not of works, but of him that calleth" (Romans 9:11, KJV). A child, after coming to what's called "the age of accountability," has a lifetime to repent and find God. A patient God wants you. You matter to Him. He wants the love of free men, not the fearful adoration of slaves.

Aren't I important? If God doesn't exist, I'm pointless! How often at a funeral, the only solace offered is "We'll remember him." Sure, at times I'll be remembered by loved ones . . . but after a few generations I'm totally forgotten. Still, God remembers. Jesus' parable shows us our importance: "Suppose one of you has a hundred sheep and loses one of them. Does he not leave the ninety-nine . . . and go after the lost sheep until he finds it . . . Then he calls his friends and neighbors together and says, 'Rejoice with me; I have found my lost sheep.' I tell you that in the same way there will be more rejoicing in heaven over one sinner who repents . . ." (Luke 15:4-7).

Because we're born outside Eden, we must find and embrace God's plan to bring us back in His presence. If we choose to reject Him, He won't override the free will He gave us.

My choice is to decide which higher power I'll serve. Will you serve the Creator God or a demon god or idol? A demon may appear as a beautiful angel, or an astral guide. " . . . Satan himself masquerades as an angel of light. It is not surprising, then, if his servants masquerade as servants of righteousness" (2 Corinthians 11:14, 15). If we dabble in mysticism, we will encounter evil higher powers.

Satan tempted Jesus saying, "'All this I will give you,' he said, 'if you will bow down and worship me." Jesus said, "Away from me, Satan! For it is written: 'Worship the Lord your God, and serve him only'" (Matthew 4:9, 10).

God's foreknowledge of His children isn't favoritism— just that He knows in advance, who will reject Him. Don't perish! There's no reason to remain spiritually dead!

PRAY: *"Help me realize the urgency of my peril and the unfailing patience of Your mercy."*

DAY 07 — DAYBREAK The Fall (from Heaven).

READING:

"You [Satan] were blameless in your ways from the day you were created till wickedness was found in you. Through your widespread trade you were filled with violence, and you sinned. So I drove you in disgrace from the mount of God, and I expelled you, O guardian cherub, from among the fiery stones. Your heart became proud on account of your beauty, and you corrupted your wisdom because of your splendor. So I threw you to the earth; I made a spectacle of you before kings . . . I reduced you to ashes on the ground in the sight of all who were watching. All the nations who knew you are appalled at you; you have come to a horrible end and will be no more" (Ezekiel 28:15-19).

"I [Jesus] saw Satan fall like lightning from heaven" (Luke 10:18).

ENCOUNTER

Enter Michael, robed in brilliant white, now locked in armed combat with a ghoulish creature. The two titans shudder in each other's grip. The archangel in white turns and throws the demon off balance. The devil rolls a moment. He hesitates just enough to be hurled over the battleground, past the horizon into space, until he crashes on the earth.

Before men existed, there was an upheaval of giant proportions. A mutiny of delinquents against loyal spirits rocked the foundations of heaven. Not confined to physical boundaries or time, the clash might have lasted eons.

Pride, wanting to be as God, gave the dark powers confidence to try to overthrow the Eternal One. The Almighty empowered trustworthy forces and the rebellion was defeated.

Heaven banished Satan and other demonic angels to the earth and the netherworld. Someday evil spirits will be completely neutralized.

"And the angels who did not keep their positions of authority but abandoned their own home— these he has kept in darkness, bound with everlasting chains for judgment on the great Day" (Jude 1:6).

". . . God did not spare angels when they sinned, but sent them to hell, putting them into gloomy dungeons to be held for judgment" (2 Peter 2:4).

Fierce combat between good and evil persists today. Invisible confrontations go on all around us. The battles will continue until the end of time. Spiritual forces in exile on earth have influenced evil in and upon humans since the Great Fall.

PRAY: *"God, protect me from the evil of fallen powers."*

DAY 07 — SUNDOWN The Fall (on Earth).

READING

"And the LORD God said, 'The man has now become like one of us, knowing good and evil. He must not be allowed to reach out his hand and take also from the tree of life and eat, and live forever.' So the LORD God banished him from the Garden of Eden to work the ground from which he had been taken" (Genesis 3:22, 23).

ENCOUNTER

Before the ground was cursed, Eden was like a glorious greenhouse. There were fruit trees of lemon, orange, pear, and apple. There probably were poppies, daffodils, tulips, and perennial flowers of sun and shade. Breezes rippled the grain fields. There were no weeds, thorns, or thistles. Bees without stingers feasted on honeysuckle. Even the mighty lion was harmless. Instead of rain, a mist watered the ground. A river ran through Eden feeding brooks, waterfalls, and clear pools.

God gave man, Adam, care for His entire garden. Adam also named the animals and sea creatures. He could feed them by hand for sheer enjoyment. This idyllic life, however, was short-lived.

Adam and Eve, the first humans created in God's image, fell to pride, just like Satan. Satan enticed them to want to be "like God," having unlimited knowledge, saying, "For God knows that when you eat of it your eyes will be opened, and you will be like God, knowing good and evil" (Genesis 3:5). They were disinherited after eating from "the Tree of the knowledge of good and evil." God posted an angel at the entrance to block permanently the way back to Eden.

Physical and spiritual death was born at humanity's fall. " . . . As sin entered the world through one man [Adam], and death through sin, and in this way death came to all men, because all sinned" (Romans 5:12).

Women would experience pain in childbirth (Genesis 3:16). Men would be forced to work (Genesis 3:19). In one generation Adam and Eve's sons committed violence as Cain slaughtered his brother Abel. Disease flourished. Man's lifespan began to shorten.

You say, "I don't want to believe in a God who allows pain and suffering." We, like Adam, choose to sin, and to keep on doing it! These consequences weren't in God's perfect plan. There was no anguish in the Garden. Satan fell, and man fell!

It's not what you do, it's what you were at birth. You were born damaged. And it's what you are. Haven't you ever wondered why God seems aloof or nonexistent in your life? You call to Him but there's no answer. That's because ". . . your iniquities have separated you from your God; your sins have hidden his face from you, so that he will not hear" (Isaiah 59:2).

Let God make you right. Turn to God to fix you. The dilemma we must answer is, how does exiled man return to Paradise?

PRAY: *"Return me to the beauty of Your safe garden."*

DAY 08 — DAYBREAK Evil (outside us).

READING

"One day the angels came to present themselves before the Lord, and Satan also came with them. The LORD said to Satan, 'Where have you come from?' Satan answered the LORD, 'From roaming through the earth and going back and forth in it'" (Job 1:6, 7).

"The evening meal was being served, and the devil had already prompted Judas Iscariot, son of Simon, to betray Jesus" (John 13:2).

ENCOUNTER

Fallen powers of darkness inhabit the occult, psychic phenomena, metaphysics, astrology, wizardry, poltergeists, clairvoyance, voodoo, witchcraft, demonology, possession, conjuring, spiritual guides, and so on. These disciplines are grounded in Satanism. They undermine our loyalty to God and can get total control of us.

Satan, cast from heaven, walks the earth. Yet, he has access to God's presence to accuse us. He appears sometimes as light, sometimes evil, and at times he's an unseen force. Satan and company oppress us, "For our struggle is not against flesh and blood, but against the rulers, against the authorities, against the powers of this dark world and against the spiritual forces of evil in the heavenly realms" (Ephesians 6:12).

You can't fight superior spiritual forces except through a greater power. Come under God's shelter! He offers protection for His children, as stated in Colossians 1:13, "For he has rescued us from the dominion of darkness and brought us into the kingdom of the Son he loves."

God warns us to flee from evil people or beings. "Let no one be found among you who sacrifices his son or daughter in the fire, who practices divination or sorcery, interprets omens, engages in witchcraft, or casts spells, or who is a medium or spiritist or who consults the dead. Anyone who does these things is detestable to the LORD . . ." (Deuteronomy 18:10-12).

Cry out to God and His light will overcome the blackness that traps you. And thank God for ministers and priests experienced at calling on God's power, in Jesus' name, to defeat and exorcise harassing spirits. Jesus told Simon Peter, noted in Luke 22:31, "Satan has asked to sift you as wheat. But I have prayed for you, Simon . . .".

Call out Christ's name and He will deliver you from the occult. Jesus delivered people when He was on earth, and even more so now, in heaven, He continues to rescue us. "That at the name of Jesus every knee should bow, in heaven and on earth and under the earth" (Philippians 2:10).

PRAY: *"I've turned away from You. I've cursed You at times, my Creator. I've spit in Your face. I've worshiped false gods, people, heavenly bodies, animals, wealth, and spirit beings. Now it seems I can't be loosed from my bonds. Help me find my way back to freedom. I'm powerless without You. In the Name of Jesus, please release me from evil, please help me!"*

DAY 08 — SUNDOWN Evil (within us).

READING

"The heart is deceitful above all things, and beyond cure . . ." (Jeremiah 17:9).

"The hearts of men . . . are full of evil, and there is madness in their hearts" (Ecclesiastes 9:3).

ENCOUNTER

Evil is like a seed planted in the brain. Nourished by the imagination, increasing to full flower in the mind, sin takes root, travels fast to the heart, and absorbs the soul.

A consequence of man's fall is to know and to do evil. Dark forces want us to commit every evil deed. Without God, man's heart and mind craves, and would indulge in, every depravity. Both love and evil spring from the heart. In Mark 7:21-22 Jesus proclaims man's evil nature: "For from within, out of men's hearts, come evil thoughts, sexual immorality, theft, murder, adultery, greed, malice, deceit, lewdness, envy, slander, arrogance and folly."

Kidnapping, murder, fraud, theft, serial killings, genocide, hindering relief efforts, forced starvation, terrorism, slavery, sexual abuse, spiritual bondage and spiritual abuse—all are examples of great evil. We deceive ourselves if we think we can't commit those acts. The evidence of history says otherwise.

Your will can barely overcome the evil that wages war against you— against Satan, the enemy from without, and against the traitor from within (the heart). We live under the control of our own desires. Let God battle the evil in your world, for a human's frail will is hopeless to defeat supernatural forces and the longings of the heart.

Every religion but Christianity says that man is capable of improving, even reaching perfection, and that "the good" may attain the utmost. Yet, God recognizes and provides for our weaknesses and our evil nature by forgiving human frailty. God Himself is the standard for righteousness; humans always disappoint. He says, "Be holy because I, the LORD your God, am holy" (Leviticus 19:2).

Does God raise a standard that humans cannot reach? Yes, exactly! The paradox is— no one can reach God's standard. On one hand, God says man is fallen, sinful, incorrigible, defiant, corrupt, and depraved. On the other, God created people and saw that His creation was good.

"But I'm a moral person. My sins are only small ones." Christianity says that everyone needs God's power to overcome evil, to change our thoughts, our heart, our behavior, and to receive forgiveness. Jesus isn't only for maximum-security prisoners but for all people. Life is total hell without Christ. If God doesn't intervene, I'm doomed!

Yet, God gives us an out. He wants to overlook, forgive, and forget. Then He works to change us and repair our weaknesses. Addiction can be healed. Mental illness can be corrected. Emotions can be made stable. Broken lives can be fixed.

PRAY: *"God, help me to escape the evil that controls me from without. And help me overcome the open Pandora's box inside me that keeps me from doing good."*

DAY 09 — DAYBREAK Sin.

READING

"There is not a righteous man on earth who does what is right and never sins" (Ecclesiastes 7:20).

"All have sinned and fall short of the glory of God" (Romans 3:23).

ENCOUNTER

What is God like? His glory is the expression of radiant holiness. His attributes are beyond us. "For whoever keeps the whole law and yet stumbles at just one point is guilty of breaking all of it" (James 2:10). Sin is falling short of God's perfect standards and can be a measure of our discontent and dissatisfaction with God. Sin is separation from God. Don't compare your goodness to that of other people, but to a holy God. Good people don't inhabit heaven—only perfect people do.

We received genes from imperfect parents, our upbringing was flawed, and we're bent by life's traumas. And negative spiritual inheritance passes between generations like a curse. The Lord is ". . . a jealous God, punishing the children for the sin of the fathers to the third and fourth generation of those who hate me, but showing love to a thousand generations of those who love me and keep my commandments" (Deuteronomy 5:9, 10).

It's no surprise that we fail at perfect morality and spirituality, as we can't be perfect on our own. This may sound familiar. "Nothing good lives in me, that is, in my sinful nature. For I have the desire to do what is good, but I cannot carry it out. For what I do is not the good I want to do; no, the evil I do not want to do— this I keep on doing" (Romans 7:18, 19). You're born "dead in your transgressions and sins" (Ephesians 2:1). We expect man to want to do good. God knows that we can't, ". . . for he knew what was in a man" (John 2:25).

It seems the further along the spiritual path we travel, the stronger the pull of sin. Yet, God's grace increases to meet our trials. In J. R. R. Tolkien's Return of the King, Frodo felt the growing pull of darkness as he neared the source. Climbing Mount Doom, the Ring he had to destroy became an unbearable weight.

Like the burden of Frodo's Ring, the stress of sin to your body, soul, and mind can become unbearable weights. We don't— and we can't— measure up to God's standard. We sin and can't stop. Adam and Eve failed and their children failed, too. Yet, God's Spirit, indwelling in us, can brace our wills to conquer sin. Christ defeated the penalty for sin and defeated the influence of sin.

Biblical law wasn't written because God expects men to be perfect. After all, there are over six hundred laws, rites, and thus penalties in the Old Covenant. Instead, He gave the law to show it's impossible to be moral without His help. ". . . I would not have known what sin was except through the law. For I would not have known what coveting really was if the law had not said, 'Do not covet'" (Romans 7:7). He also provides the law for our benefit, as Deuteronomy 10:13 says, "Observe the Lord's commands and decrees that I am giving you today for your own good . . .".

PRAY: *"I need to see that I'm not righteous and never will be. What a relief that I was never expected to perform perfectly; that You prefer to help me and not destroy me."*

DAY 09 — SUNDOWN Sin.

READING

". . . Everything . . . the cravings of sinful man, the lust of his eyes and the boasting of what he has and does— comes not from the Father but from the world" (1 John 2:16).

" . . . There is no one who understands, no one who seeks God" (Romans 3:11).

ENCOUNTER

The human form is the most beautiful, sensuous, and desirable of God's physical masterpieces. The skin— white, pink, beige, tan, red, yellow, ebony—is a supple, living organism stretched masterfully over a delicate frame of fine bone, like living china. Smooth, soft, firm, or hard, flesh longs to be touched and to touch.

Hair is radiant with its hues of shining brown, blue-black, raven black, blonde, red, auburn, and chestnut. Voices of bass, tenor, or alto can be soothing and tender. Eyes like jewels flash one's personality. My flesh calls out to the flesh of others, like the moon pulling on the tides. Prone to disobedience, sin holds our inner true selves imprisoned in flesh.

Temptation often exceeds our will to resist. Yet, we're warned to obey, to keep our thoughts and our bodies clean, and not give in to sexual desires. We're commanded not to commit adultery, covet our neighbor's spouse, or worship the god of the body! Jesus raised the level of sin from actions to motives of the heart. He likened murder to anger, and adultery to lust.

Gluttony is the flesh's desire for food beyond sustaining life. The search for exotic dishes and rare wines inflames but never satisfies the appetite that panders to the senses of smell and taste. Our eyes desire the world's riches and luxuries, the rainbow captured in a diamond, and the glint of gold. We want what we see. Solomon, the wealthiest of men lamented in Ecclesiastes 2:10, 11, "I denied myself nothing my eyes desired; I refused my heart no pleasure . . . when I surveyed all that my hands had done and what I had toiled to achieve, everything was meaningless . . .".

". . . But the one who is rich . . . he will pass away like a wild flower. For the sun rises with scorching heat and withers the plant; its blossom falls and its beauty is destroyed. In the same way, the rich man will fade away even while he goes about his business" (James 1:10, 11).

Pride exalts self. Arrogance won't submit to the authority of the greatest power. "I'll do it myself." "I can win without God." "I'm king of my own universe." "I'll get to heaven on my own goodness." Pride was Satan's fatal error. ". . . You have fallen from heaven, O morning star, [Lucifer] son of the dawn! . . . You said in your heart, 'I will ascend to heaven; I will raise my throne above the stars of God . . . I will make myself like the Most High" (Isaiah 14:12-14). Pride and rebelliousness are sins that God hates. "Haughty eyes and a proud heart, the lamp of the wicked, are sin!" (Proverbs 21:4).

". . . God opposes the proud but gives grace to the humble" (James 4:6). God is so innately holy that He cannot tolerate any sin. Thankfully, God makes a way for us to escape sin and its penalty.

PRAY: *"How did I fall into the trap of sin? Show me my sins that I may turn from them."*

DAY 10 — DAYBREAK The Purpose.

READING

"But when the time had fully come, God sent His Son, born of a woman, born under law, to redeem those under law, that we might receive the full rights of sons" (Galatians 4:4, 5).

"[Jesus] by the grace of God he might taste death for everyone. In bringing many sons to glory, it was fitting that God, for whom and through whom everything exists, should make the author of their salvation perfect through suffering" (Hebrews 2:9, 10).

"The creation waits in eager expectation for the sons of God to be revealed" (Romans 8:19).

"Thou hast created all things, and for thy pleasure they are and were created" (Revelation 4:11, KJV).

"A chosen people, a royal priesthood, a holy nation, a people belonging to God . . . declare the praises of him who called you out of darkness into his wonderful light" (1 Peter 2:9, 10).

"But our citizenship is in heaven. And we eagerly await a Savior from there, the Lord Jesus Christ" (Philippians 3:20, 21).

". . . The God of all grace, who called you to his eternal glory in Christ . . ." (1 Peter 5:10).

ENCOUNTER

God wants many children. He's creating a holy nation, a Kingdom of sons and daughters, and His design will be completed. The universe won't end until all generations of God's children experience Eternal Life (through the new birth) and receive an immortal body after death.

The tie between a Christian and Christ is like a marriage. He's the Bridegroom; Christians are called the "Body of Christ" or the "Bride." ". . . Be married to another, even to him who is raised from the dead, that we should bring forth fruit unto God" (Romans 7:4, KJV).

The prophet Daniel stated the purpose for the coming Messiah, saying in Daniel 9:24, the time would come ". . . to finish transgression, to put an end to sin, to atone for wickedness, to bring in everlasting righteousness, to seal up vision and prophecy and to anoint the most holy." The moment for Jesus to appear arrived without pomp. He fulfilled Daniel's prophecies by taking on Himself the penalty of man's sin.

Jesus rescues us from the full weight of the law. He paid to make us God's children, sinless and eligible to wear the mantle of royalty. He's for everyone! Anyone can be transformed by God's Son and made heaven-bound.

God's pleasure, His desire, is that we receive all He prepared for us. "The Son of Man did not come to be served, but to serve, and to give his life as a ransom for many" (Matthew 20:28). He came to give, not to take! All is by Him and for Him, and for me.

PRAY: *"What is the purpose of life, and of my life?"*

DAY 10 — SUNDOWN The Purpose.

READING

"God who made the world and everything in it is the Lord of heaven and earth and does not live in temples built by hands. And he is not served by human hands, as if he needed anything, because he himself gives all men life and breath and everything else. From one man he made every nation of men, that they should inhabit the whole earth; and he determined the times set for them and the exact places where they should live. God did this so that men would seek him and perhaps reach out for him and find him, though he is not far from each one of us. For in him we live and move and have our being . . . 'We are his offspring'" (Acts 17:24-28).

". . . The true worshipers will worship the Father in spirit and truth; for they are the kind of worshipers the Father seeks. God is spirit, and his worshipers must worship in spirit and in truth" (John 4:23, 24).

". . . Chosen by God and precious to him— you also, like living stones, are being built into a spiritual house to be a holy priesthood, offering spiritual sacrifices acceptable to God through Jesus Christ" (1 Peter 2:4, 5).

". . . Worship him who made the heavens, the earth, the sea and the springs of water" (Revelation 14:7).

"Who will not fear you, O Lord, and bring glory to your name? For you alone are holy. All nations will come and worship before you . . ." (Revelation 15:4).

"We belong to the Lord. For this very reason, Christ died and returned to life so that he might be the Lord of both the dead and the living" (Romans 14:8, 9).

". . . Receiving a kingdom that cannot be shaken . . . so worship God acceptably with reverence and awe, for our God is a consuming fire" (Hebrews 12:28, 29).

". . . Whether you eat or drink or whatever . . . do it all for the glory of God" (1 Corinthians 10:31).

ENCOUNTER

We're brought to God, and salvation through faith, to HONOR and OBEY Him, WORSHIP and ADORE Him, REVERE, GLORIFY, and SERVE HIM and to be loved by Him. He showed me His love for me by creating me.

We're not preprogrammed. We're not machines. We may choose freely to accept or reject the Redeemer. We didn't choose our father and mother and probably don't hate them for conceiving and for raising us. We love them unconditionally. So why despise God for existing, for being our Maker?

Once we grasp our purpose in life, that we may have a relationship with the heavenly Creator, we're free to love Him!

PRAY: *"There's something in me that wants to resist Your omnipotence. I need to submit to the reality that, even as my parents participated in my creation, You made them and me."*

DAY 11 — DAYBREAK The Birth.

READING

"This is how the birth of Jesus Christ came about: His mother Mary was pledged to be married to Joseph, but before they came together, she was found to be with child through the Holy Spirit" (Matthew 1:18).

"But he [Joseph] had no union with her until she gave birth to a son" (Matthew 1:25).

"You will be with child and give birth to a son, and you are to give him the name Jesus . . . and will be called the Son of the Most High. The Lord God will give him the throne of his father David" . . . "'How will this be,' Mary asked the angel, 'since I am a virgin?' The angel answered, 'The Holy Spirit will come upon you, and the power of the Most High will overshadow you. So the holy one . . . will be called the Son of God'" (Luke 1:31-35).

ENCOUNTER

Jesus was born of one human parent, His mother Mary (Miriam). The Bible says that she never knew a man, that she and Joseph abstained from sex. When God asked Mary's permission, through an angel, to bear God's Son, she agreed. With delicate intimacy, God's seed, His Holy Spirit, was planted in Mary's womb and thus God the Son, "the Word," took on flesh.

The union of God and woman was the Son of God. Jesus had to be both human and divine! "The Word became flesh and made his dwelling among us . . . who came from the Father" (John 1:14). God spoke to Satan just after the fall of Man, saying, "And I will put enmity between you and the woman, and between your offspring and hers; he [Messiah] will crush your [the Serpent's] head, and you will strike his heel" (Genesis 3:15). Jesus is the only person in history born only of a woman. And Jesus is Satan's adversary.

"The virgin [*Parthenos*, Greek] will be with child and will give birth to a son, and they will call him Immanuel"— which means, 'God with us'" (Matthew 1:23). The New Testament Greek word for virgin is *Parthenos*. Isaiah predicted the virgin birth hundreds of years before Jesus, ". . . the Lord himself will give you a <u>sign</u>: The virgin [*Almah*, Hebrew] will be with child and will give birth to a son, and will call him Immanuel" (Isaiah 7:14, emphasis mine).

Since the Hebrew word *Almah* may be translated as either young girl or virgin, why do Christians assume virgin and not maiden? Because a maiden giving birth isn't a sign, but a virgin giving birth surely is one! Also, the Septuagint, a pre-Christ Greek translation of the Old Covenant, translated the Hebrew word *Almah* into the Greek [*Parthenos*] in Isaiah 7:14 *Parthenos* has only one meaning: It's always translated virgin!

So, before Christ was born, scholars knew the prediction of a virgin birth. Mary conceived a child in the likeness of Man, yet fully God at the incarnation, "*en karnos*," or taking on flesh. Jesus received only one set of chromosomes, those from His mother. The other chromosomes must have been of the Holy Spirit. God chose to be born as a man instead of intruding on earth as a spirit or an alien being. The incarnation began to fulfill His plan to reveal sons and daughters.

PRAY: *"A virgin giving birth is literally inconceivable. Help me to consider the possibility, and to understand the reason."*

DAY 11 — SUNDOWN The Birth.

READING

"Today in the town of David a Savior has been born to you; he is Christ the Lord. This will be a sign to you: You will find a baby wrapped in cloths and lying in a manger" (Luke 2:11).

ENCOUNTER

King Herod asked where the Messiah would be born. The priests and scribes replied, "Bethlehem," quoting this Old Covenant prophecy. "Bethlehem . . . out of thee shall he come forth unto me that is to be ruler in Israel; whose goings forth have been from of old, from everlasting" (Micah 5:2, KJV). Rabbi Jarchi interprets Micah 5:2 as follows: "Out of thee (Bethlehem) shall come forth unto me Messiah, the Son of David." [4] Because Herod believed the Messiah was born, he ordered that every Bethlehem boy less than two years old be killed. Jesus was spared an early death when Mary and Joseph hid Him in Egypt.

The Messiah's origins are from before time, but here is His earthly pedigree:

A descendant of Abraham: ". . . He took on him the Seed of Abraham" (Hebrews 2:16, KJV). An heir of Jacob: "A star will come out of Jacob; a scepter will rise out of Israel" (Numbers 24:17). A descendant of Jacob's son, Judah: "The sceptre shall not depart from Judah . . . until Shiloh come; and unto him shall the gathering of the people be" (Genesis 49:10, KJV). *Shiloh* "to whom it belongs," implies Messiah. In Revelation 5:5, Christ is called the "Lion of the Tribe of Judah, the Root of David."

An heir of King David: ". . . I will raise up to David a righteous Branch [Hebrew *Netzer* or Nazarene], a King who will reign wisely . . . The LORD Our Righteousness" (Jeremiah 23:5, 6). The word branch in Hebrew is *Netzer*, perhaps an obscure reference in the Old Covenant to Nazareth, the town where Jesus grew up.

The lineage of Jesus' stepfather Joseph, in Matthew 1, shows that Joseph came from King David and Solomon. ". . . Joseph the husband, of Mary, of whom was born Jesus, who is called Christ" (Matthew 1:1, 2, and Matthew 1:16, KJV). Yet, Joseph's lineage is irrelevant as he wasn't Jesus' father. In Joseph's line (Matthew 1:11) was the accursed King Jechonias, not destined to be part of the line for Messiah (Jeremiah 22:24-30).

Joseph was Mary's husband but he wasn't Jesus' father. Jesus fulfilled the Messianic lineage of his mother Mary as found in Luke 3. She was a descendant of Abraham through Judah and a descendant of King David through David's son Nathan (2 Samuel 5:14). If Messiah were to come today, we can't know if He's descended from King David through Judah. Tribal records existed in Jesus' day, but were lost through the dispersion of the Jewish people.

Jewish tradition claims two advents of Messiah—Messiah ben (son of) Joseph, and Messiah ben (son of) David. Messiah ben Joseph, called the "Suffering Messiah," is Jesus at His crucifixion. Messiah ben David, known as the "Victorious Messiah," will be Jesus Christ at His return to earth as He predicted.

PRAY: *"That Jesus fulfilled the Old Covenant requirement of Messiah's lineage seems overwhelming. Please make Jesus real to me. Show me if He's the Messiah."*

DAY 12 — DAYBREAK The Miracles.

READING

". . . The kingdom of heaven is near. Heal the sick, raise the dead, cleanse those who have leprosy, drive out demons . . ." (Matthew 10:7, 8).

"Jesus called in a loud voice, 'Lazarus, come out!' The dead man came out, his hands and feet wrapped with strips of linen, and a cloth around his face. Jesus said to them, 'Take off the grave clothes and let him go'" (John 11:43, 44).

ENCOUNTER

The people of the small town of Bethany mourned for Lazarus after he prematurely died of an illness. They placed a stone over the cave tomb where he lay buried four days.

With Lazarus gone, the faith of the townspeople was weak. But hope is a flickering flame. When Jesus arrived, He renewed their hope, for the Son of God is mighty in word and deed. Could Jesus raise Lazarus from the dead?

Mary and Martha felt that Jesus could have healed Lazarus before their brother died, so they nearly scold Jesus. True, Jesus delayed His return to Bethany even after hearing of Lazarus' death.

The Master felt deeply for He loved Lazarus and He cried from an eternal pain. The Bible states that, "Jesus wept" (John 11:35). Then He said, "Take away the stone!" (John 11:39). Lifting His eyes to heaven, He called out to His Father with faith to loose death's grip, saying, "Lazarus, come out!" (John 11:43). Lazarus staggered from the vault bound in grave clothes.

Jesus restored Lazarus from death. Who restores life but the Author of life?

Many believed in Jesus after this miracle and Lazarus became a rarity, a celebrity. Jesus' enemies conspired to kill Lazarus for, as a living witness, he turned people to Jesus.

". . . A large crowd of Jews found out that Jesus was there and came, not only because of him but also to see Lazarus, whom he had raised from the dead. So the chief priests made plans to kill Lazarus as well, for on account of him many of the Jews were going over to Jesus and putting their faith in him" (John 12:9-11).

These events foreshadowed Jesus' own Resurrection and that of His followers and they give us hope for Eternal Life.

PRAY: *"I've little hope beyond the grave, though You're a glimmer of hope. Have mercy on me as You did with Lazarus. Love me as You did Lazarus."*

DAY 12 — SUNDOWN The Miracles.

READING

"But the boat was already a considerable distance from land, buffeted by the waves because the wind was against it. During the fourth watch of the night Jesus went out to them, walking on the lake" (Matthew 14:24).

"When they had rowed three or three and a half miles, they saw Jesus approaching the boat, walking on the water and they were terrified. But He said to them, 'It is I; don't be afraid'" (John 6:19, 20).

ENCOUNTER

The wind whipped the waves of the Sea of Galilee into breakers, boiling the tops into emerald gray foam. The gale sounded like muted sirens or ten thousand penny whistles. Although the apostles were out of sight of land, Jesus saw them clearly, struggling in the early morning tempest.

Jesus marched to them on the sea as if the water were a solid. The sea splashed from his ankles up past the knees. Striding on the rough surface, the natural laws were arrested for a time. Job said of Him in Job 9:8, "He . . . treads on the waves of the sea." Who walks on the ocean? Who can suspend physical laws? Only God can.

The apostles were afraid, thinking he was a ghost from the deep. He said to them, in Matthew 14:27, ". . . Be of good cheer; it is I; be not afraid." He walked to the boat, entered, and the wind ceased. In the vessel, they worshipped the Son of God.

Peter had walked, too. ". . . Then Peter got down out of the boat, walked on the water and came toward Jesus. But when he saw the wind, he was afraid and, beginning to sink, cried out, "Lord, save me!" (Matthew 14:29, 30).

Peter proved that man could overcome the elements through faith in God, though Peter faltered after a few moments. Jesus asked him, in Matthew 14:31, ". . . 'You of little faith,' he said, 'why did you doubt?'" Yet, no other man has ever negotiated the surface of water like Peter.

When they arrived at the opposite shore, everyone in Capernaum knew Jesus didn't begin the journey in the boat and that He miraculously caught up to the disciples.

Three Gospels report this story. If the account were a lie, the followers wouldn't admit their fear of their boat sinking, or their fear of the apparition of their own leader. Many biblical accounts are fantastic, yet the honesty of the witnesses makes the events sound plausible.

PRAY: *"This account seems impossible, yet the story has the ring of truth. God, I want to believe in You as the power greater than me."*

DAY 13 — DAYBREAK The Miracles.

READING

"A man . . . possessed by an evil spirit cried out, 'What do you want with us, Jesus of Nazareth? . . . I know who you are— the Holy One of God!' 'Be quiet!' said Jesus sternly. 'Come out of him!' The evil spirit shook the man violently and came out of him with a shriek" (Mark 1:23-26).

"If I drive out demons by the finger of God, then the kingdom of God has come . . ." (Luke 11:20).

ENCOUNTER

New Age philosophies and psychic exploits compete with worship of God. When we rebel from God, spiritual warfare from demonic forces heightens. Multiple evil spirits lived in the man that Jesus healed. God's Holy Spirit in a person's life will protect him from dark spirits.

Using deep meditation, taking "walks" with astral (spiritual) guides, participating in cults, reading occult literature, consulting clairvoyants, witches, and psychic advisors, listening to satanic music or watching movies that glorify Satan and death, praying to Satan, or participating in satanic ritual are all ways we open ourselves to spiritual attack. Drugs or alcohol may initiate one's bondage and substance abuse intensifies one's oppression.

Jesus often cast out demons from the possessed, in exorcism. Jesus used different techniques or tools to exorcise spirits:

His Voice. "He drove out the spirits with a word and healed all the sick" (Matthew 8:16). "He said to them, 'Go!'" (Matthew 8:32). ". . . He rebuked the evil spirit. 'You deaf and mute spirit,' he said, 'I command you, come out of him and never enter him again'" (Mark 9:25).

The Holy Spirit. ". . . I drive out demons by the Spirit of God, then the kingdom of God has come upon you" (Matthew 12:28).

By Prayer and Fasting. ". . . This kind goeth not out but by prayer and fasting" (Matthew 17:21, KJV).

By Silencing. "'Be quiet!' said Jesus sternly. 'Come out of him!'" (Mark 1:25).

By Sight. "Whenever the evil spirits saw him, they fell down before him and cried out, 'You are the Son of God'" (Mark 3:11).

By Touch. ". . . Laying his hands on each one, he healed them . . ." (Luke 4:40).

Turn to God and be free from the occult. God's power will loose Satan's grip and relieve one from demons. Jesus' followers exorcise spirits when done in Jesus' name. Paul said to the spirit, "In the name of Jesus Christ I command you to come out of her! At that moment the spirit left her" (Acts 16:18). Say the name of Jesus to release divine power against demonic oppression.

PRAY: *"I remember my childhood when life seemed simple. I could look at the sky and know that somehow God was watching over me. Now I feel oppressed and depressed. Lord, lift my burdens and return me to that simplicity again."*

DAY 13 — SUNDOWN The Miracles.

READING

". . . A man came along who was covered with leprosy. When he saw Jesus, he fell with his face to the ground and begged him, 'Lord, if you are willing, you can make me clean.' Jesus reached out his hand and touched the man. 'I am willing,' he said. 'Be clean!' And immediately the leprosy left him" (Luke 5:12, 13).

ENCOUNTER

When the leprous man begged Jesus for mercy Jesus healed him. Jesus moved among the untouchables and castaways and cured everyone who believed in Him.

Jesus was summoned to the town where Jairus' twelve-year-old daughter lay dying. On the journey, a messenger told Jesus that she was already dead. When Jesus said not to worry, that she would revive, the locals laughed at Him. He held the dead girl's hand and said, in Luke 8:41, "My child, get up," and she stood. No one in the town, or the dead girl herself, needed to exercise faith. The healing was all Jesus.

One woman was "unclean" for twelve years with a continuous flow of blood. All her money went to physicians but she remained sick. How many of us are losing all our savings on cures! As Jesus passed, she touched the border of His garment and was healed immediately (Luke 8:43).

He asked, "Who touched me?" Not just, who touched my clothing, but who summoned the belief in Me that touched My heart and released My healing power! The sick woman's faith in Jesus instantly released His power to make her well.

Another time a centurion summoned Jesus to his home in Capernaum because the centurion's servant was near death. The centurion sent word to Jesus not to come because of his own unworthiness. Even from a distance, he knew Jesus had the authority and the ability to heal. "I have not found such great faith," complimented the Great Physician. The servant became well (Luke 7).

God may seem remote, yet today Jesus continues to cure people at various stages of faith in Him. Jesus also wants to heal our broken hearts. He responds to our pain, problems, and tragedies. He helps us just to make it through each day. His promise is astounding: "And I will do whatever you ask in my name, so that the Son may bring glory to the Father. You may ask me for anything in my name, and I will do it" (John 14:13, 14). Jesus wants to meet our deepest needs in answer to our prayers.

Believe in Him. Be healed!

PRAY: *"Jesus, my faith in You seems so inadequate. Find my faith in You pleasing! Have mercy for I know You're good! Take my seed of faith and cause my faith to grow beyond my expectations. I'm sick, with nowhere to turn. Jesus, please heal me."*

DAY 14 — DAYBREAK The Seer.

READING

"I saw you while you were still under the fig tree before Philip called you" (John 1:48).

ENCOUNTER

Did you ever meet a person you never saw before who knew all about you? Jesus, a prophet and a seer, was that sort of Person. In the passage just quoted, He knew all about Nathan.

Nathan (also called Bartholomew) was an apostle. Friend of and perhaps brother to the better-known Philip (John 1:45), Nathan lived in Cana where Jesus would soon turn water into the finest reserve wine (John 21:2). Philip told Nathan that he'd discovered a very special person called Jesus. "We have found the one Moses wrote about in the Law and about whom the prophets also wrote . . ." (John 1:45). Skeptical at first, Nathan asked, in John 1:46, "Nazareth! Can anything good come from there?"

When Nathan finally met Him, Jesus related Nathan's thoughts. Jesus made Nathan understand that He saw him, through space and time, seated under a fig tree. Jesus sees inside us to the core of the brain, to the chambers of the heart. "He knew all men . . . He knew what was in a man" (John 2:24, 25). Faced with Jesus' improbable knowledge, and prepared by Philip, Nathan believed in Jesus. He said, in John 1:49, "Rabbi, you are the Son of God; you are the King of Israel."

Jesus told Nathan even greater things. ". . . You shall see heaven open, and the angels of God ascending and descending on the Son of Man" (John 1:51). Later, Nathan and Philip would travel to India to preach and they met death by flaying and upside-down crucifixion.

Andrew told his brother, Simon Peter, about Jesus. "We have found the Messiah . . ." (John 1:41). Impetuous Peter, courageous Peter, the one who defended His Master in the Garden of Gethsemane. His Lord knew Him intimately but also could see ahead. Jesus predicted that Peter would be unfaithful: ". . . I tell you, Peter, before the rooster crows today, you will deny three times that you know me" (Luke 22:34). Peter's unfaithfulness is recorded in Luke 22:57-60.

1. "Woman, I don't know him [Jesus]" (Verse 57).
2. "Man, I am not [a Christian]!" (Verse 58).
3. "Man, I don't know what you're talking about [That he was with Jesus]!" (Verse 60).

Jesus told Peter that the end of his life would be difficult. ". . . When you were younger you dressed yourself and went where you wanted; but when you are old you will stretch out your hands, and someone else will dress you and lead you where you do not want to go" (John 21:18). Jesus saw ahead to Peter's upside-down crucifixion.

More than a historic celebrity, more than a prophet, Jesus knows our thoughts, emotions, conversations, and acts. He knows our future. He created us, so He knows our needs. As the One that ascended into heaven, Jesus is truly a good friend to have.

PRAY: *"Jesus, show me that You're in heaven and that You know me!"*

DAY 14 — SUNDOWN The Seer.

READING

"Jesus knew what they were thinking and asked, 'Why are you thinking these things in your hearts?'" (Luke 5:22).

ENCOUNTER

Jesus prayed in the hills until early that morning. When God prays, He moves mountains and shakes kingdoms. The Son and the Father continued in communion until midday. As the sun arced upward, Jesus came down from the heights.

As Jesus walked along the shoreline of the Sea of Galilee, the breeze might have been relentless upon His face. The sea birds, appearing to play, looked for sea life. The body of water could have been an ocean, for the other shore was hidden.

When He arrived at the synagogue in Capernaum, He cured a man with the palsy and forgave his sins. Healing on the Sabbath caused an outbreak of hostility, but forgiving sins on the day of rest was worse. The Pharisees thought He was committing blasphemy by pretending to be God, as only God forgives sin. Yet, who could deny that a man was healed?

When the service ended He read the minds of the Pharisees, "But Jesus knew what they were thinking . . ." (Luke 6:8). Into the deepest parts of the intellect, He sees the motive, attitude, will, and personality, those things hidden to everyone but God.

We're under God's scrutiny. He exposes everything we do, say, or think. On our day of judgment we'll feel like crying out for the "mountains to fall upon and crush us" to cover our naked inner being. "Nothing in all creation is hidden from God's sight. Everything is uncovered and laid bare before the eyes of him to whom we must give account" (Hebrews 4:13).

God sees at once all events that happen on the earth. In fact, He sees all events of history simultaneously with total awareness. It's said of God in Psalm 94:11, "The Lord knows the thoughts of man." He also knows the future. God communicates with men inaudibly: through miracles, improbable circumstances, or direct to the mind, heart, soul, and spirit. His Holy Spirit speaks in a "still, small, voice" or a "gentle whisper" (1 Kings 19:12).

In Samaria Jesus introduced Himself to a woman at Jacob's well who told Him personal things about herself. He'd never met her but He knew her, and said, in John 4:17, 18, "You are right when you say you have no husband. The fact is, you have had five husbands. . . . 'Sir,' the woman said, 'I can see that you are a prophet.'" Then He told her more things that she'd done in her life.

Jesus saw ahead to the destruction of the temple in Jerusalem. He said to His disciples in Matthew 24:2, ". . . Not one stone here will be left on another; every one will be thrown down." History records that the Romans destroyed the temple in A.D. 70, nearly forty years after Jesus' crucifixion.

PRAY: *"Jesus, if You know me, if You can read my thoughts, tell me!"*

DAY 15 — DAYBREAK The Prophecies Fulfilled.

READING

"He was despised and rejected by men . . . familiar with suffering . . . from whom men hide their faces he was despised, and we esteemed him not. Surely he took up our infirmities and carried our sorrows, yet we considered him stricken by God, smitten by him, and afflicted. But he was pierced for our transgressions, he was crushed for our iniquities; the punishment that brought us peace was upon him, and by his wounds we are healed. We all, like sheep, have gone astray, each of us has turned to his own way; and the LORD has laid on him the iniquity of us all" (Isaiah 53:3-6).

ENCOUNTER

Jesus fulfilled Isaiah's prophecy that described the first coming of the Messiah. It's said Jesus fulfilled over three hundred messianic prophecies. He even predicted His own death and Resurrection: "Destroy this temple [body], and I will raise it again in three days" (John 2:19).

The authorities recognized Jesus' power, but they wouldn't accept Him as Messiah. ". . . The chief priests, the teachers of the law and the elders mocked him. 'He saved others,' they said, 'but he can't save himself! He's the King of Israel! Let him come down now from the cross, and we will believe in him. He trusts in God. Let God rescue him now if he wants him,' for he said, 'I am the Son of God'" (Matthew 27:41 - 43). The religious leaders admitted that Jesus rescued others miraculously and that He claimed to be God's Son.

Jesus said that He fulfilled Moses' prophesy about Messiah, written in Deuteronomy 18:15: "The LORD your God will raise up for you a prophet like me from among your own brothers. You must listen to him." Jesus provoked a stoning, which He eluded, by saying, "Do not think I will accuse you before the Father. Your accuser is Moses, on whom your hopes are set. If you believed Moses, you would believe me, for he wrote about me. But since you do not believe what he wrote, how are you going to believe what I say?" (John 5:45-47).

This dialogue of Jesus is profound: "Your father Abraham rejoiced at the thought of seeing my day; he saw it and was glad. 'You are not yet fifty years old,' the Jews said to him, 'and you have seen Abraham!' . . . Jesus answered, 'before Abraham was born, I AM!' (John 8:56-58). Jesus equated Himself with Yahweh, Who told Moses His name, "God said to Moses, 'I AM WHO I AM. This is what you are to say to the Israelites: 'I AM has sent me to you'" (Exodus 3:14).

Jesus always had the people on His side. In the end, the masses turned on Him and His friends denied Him. Jesus knew it would happen. He came to fulfill every prophecy, even Isaiah 53 that predicted His own death. Isaiah prophesied that Messiah would be punished for humanity's sin. The road to crucifixion was a road of deprivation, insomnia, wounding, scourging, and affliction and then Jesus' brief life was sacrificed for humanity. ". . . Foxes have holes and birds of the air have nests, but the Son of Man has no place to lay his head" (Matthew 8:20).

He was crucified for all of <u>us</u>. Our sins were put on Him. Jesus said, in John 5:39-41, "You diligently study the Scriptures because you think that by them you possess eternal life. These are the Scriptures that testify about me, yet you refuse to come to me to have life."

PRAY: *"I've despised You and rejected You and what You did for me. I've wandered away from You. How can my past be erased?"*

DAY 15 — SUNDOWN The Prophecies Fulfilled.

READING

"Say to those with fearful hearts, 'Be strong, do not fear; your God will come, he will come with vengeance; with divine retribution he will come to save you.' Then will the eyes of the blind be opened and the ears of the deaf unstopped. Then will the lame leap like a deer, and the mute tongue shout for joy. Water will gush forth in the wilderness and streams in the desert" (Isaiah 35:4-6).

"The blind receive sight, the lame walk, those who have leprosy are cured, the deaf hear, the dead are raised, and the good news is preached to the poor" (Matthew 11:5).

ENCOUNTER

In the eighth century B.C., Isaiah told of the One who would come and do great miracles. Jesus spent much time in the wilderness, but when He came to town, He rescued people and forgave their sins. He also healed the sick and the crippled. What Matthew wrote shows that Jesus satisfied Isaiah's prophecy of God Who would come with power to heal.

As told in John 9:6, Jesus met a blind man. The divine sculptor mixed His spit with the Judean soil. God, who molds in destinies, placed the amalgam on the man's eyes. Sightless from birth, the man began to see. Jesus also met a deaf man who had a speech impediment. "After he took him aside, away from the crowd, Jesus put his fingers into the man's ears. Then he spit and touched the man's tongue. He looked up to heaven and with a deep sigh said to him, 'Ephphatha!' (which means, 'Be opened!')" (Mark 7:33). After the healing, the man could hear and speak.

King Agbarus of Edessa in Asia Minor, wasted from disease, wrote a letter asking Jesus to come. First-century historian Eusebius documents, ". . . I have heard the reports respecting thee and thy cures, as performed by thee without medicines and without the use of herbs. For as it's said, thou causest the blind to see again, the lame to walk, and thou cleansest the lepers, and thou castest out impure spirits and demons, and thou healest those that are tormented by long disease, and thou raisest the dead. And hearing all these things of thee, I concluded in my mind one of two things: either that thou art God, and having descended from heaven, doest these things, or else doing them, thou art the son of God." [5]

An invalid lay in the street. "When Jesus saw him lying there and learned that he had been in this condition for a long time, he asked him, 'Do you want to get well?'" (John 5:6). The question is puzzling, since a rational person will want to be cured. If the patient knows he's ill, the physician knows he wants to be well and heals him. We need to have this dialogue with God. He wants us to be free to choose physical and spiritual health. "Then Jesus said to him, 'Get up! Pick up your mat and walk.' At once the man was cured . . ." (John 5:8, 9).

Do I know my needs? Do I have faith in God's healing power and His desire and ability to use them for me? Do I realize that I can be rescued? Do I want to be transformed? Do I believe in Jesus' compassion and ability to give Eternal Life? Do you want to get well? Privately, we must answer yes or no.

PRAY: *"Yes! Of course, I want You to heal me. Yes! I want to be rescued."*

DAY 16 — DAYBREAK The Prophecies Fulfilled.

READING

"My God, my God, why hast thou forsaken me? . . . They gaped upon me with their mouths, as a ravening and a roaring lion . . . all my bones are out of joint: my heart is like wax; it is melted . . . My strength is dried up like a potsherd; and my tongue cleaveth to my jaws; and thou hast brought me into the dust of death. For dogs have compassed me; the assembly of the wicked have enclosed me; they pierced my hands and my feet. I may tell all my bones; they look and stare upon me. They part my garments among them, and cast lots . . ." (Psalm 22, KJV).

ENCOUNTER

The Psalmist looked through a window to the future and wrote his vision of the focal point of history, Jesus lifted up, His hands and feet pierced in crucifixion. Another Old Covenant prophet predicted that a centurion would pierce Jesus' side with a lance to assure that Jesus was dead. The piercing fulfilled Zechariah's vision, written before Jesus' birth, and shows the Father's lament for the brutality to His only born Son. ". . . They will look on me, the one they have pierced, and they will mourn for him as one mourns for an only child, and grieve bitterly for him as one grieves for a firstborn son" (Zechariah 12:10). Kimchi says of Zechariah's prophecy, "Our Rabbis interpret this of Messiah the son of Joseph, who shall be slain." [6]

Can someone be so warped to cause deliberately a deception that leads to his own death? Would a mere man even know Isaiah's prophecy and all other Messianic prophecies hidden in scrolls and be able to fulfill them? The existence of a bound, entire Bible occurred only many centuries later. Yet, God gave the prophets to write, what Jesus was destined to fulfill. Did the frightened disciples betray Him only to fulfill this prophecy, "Strike the shepherd, and the sheep will be scattered" (Zechariah 13:7)?

Hundreds of years before, Daniel prophesied the exact year of Messiah's birth and death and the time of the destruction of Jerusalem. Daniel used as a starting date a decree written in Nehemiah 2. Artarxerxes, in his twentieth year as King (445 B.C.), commanded that the temple in Jerusalem be rebuilt. Daniel wrote what the angel Gabriel told him, ". . . From the going forth of the commandment to restore and to build Jerusalem unto the Messiah, the Prince . . ." (Daniel 9:25, KJV) would be sixty-nine "weeks" (weeks—Hebrew *Shabua*— for groups of seven years).

That should be 483 (69 x 7) years. But using thirty-day lunar months, or 360-day biblical years, actually calculates as 476 years to the Messiah. (Please see the Appendix for more details.) Thus, 476 years after 445 B.C. (Artarxerxes' starting date) brings us to A.D. 31, the exact year of Jesus' death. The seventieth week ("seventy sevens") or final seven years of Daniel mentioned in Daniel 9:24 and Daniel 9:27 that Christians call the Tribulation, are yet to occur. (Please see the Appendix for an illustration, and more on the seventieth week of Daniel.)

Daniel saw ahead to the crucifixion of Christ and beyond to the destruction of the second temple. He predicted that Messiah would be ". . . Cut off, but not for himself; and the people of the prince that shall come shall destroy the city and the sanctuary; and the end thereof shall be with a flood . . ." (Daniel 9:26, KJV). The Messiah had to arrive and be killed (cut off) before A.D. 70 when the second temple in Jerusalem was destroyed by the Romans.

PRAY: *"The precision of Your prophecies is staggering."*

DAY 16 — SUNDOWN The Prophecies Fulfilled.

READING

" . . . The land of Zebulun and the land of Naphtali, but in the future he will honor Galilee of the Gentiles, by the way of the sea, along the Jordan— The people walking in darkness have seen a great light; on those living in the land of the shadow of death a light has dawned" (Isaiah 9:1, 2).

ENCOUNTER

Men walk in darkness if they haven't received spiritual birth. Christ shone His light onto the blackness of existence. Nazareth, Jesus' hometown, is west of the Jordan River. Christ preached and spread His light in the region of the Sea of Galilee. The towns He frequented like Capernaum, Gennesaret, Chorazin, and Tiberias are in the regions known as Zebulun and Napthali. How could Isaiah's prophecy be more exact? The prediction was fulfilled in Jesus (see Matthew 4:15, 16 and Luke 1:79). When Jesus came, He accomplished each Old Covenant prophecy perfectly.

"Light has come into the world" (John 3:19). "Arise from the dead, and Christ shall give thee light" (Ephesians 5:14, KJV). "God is light" (1 John 1:5). "A light for revelation to the Gentiles and for glory to your people Israel" (Luke 2:32). "In him was life, and that life was the light of men" (John 1:4).

Jesus said, "I am the light of the world. Whoever follows me will never walk in darkness, but will have the light of life" (John 8:12). "Then Jesus told them, 'You are going to have the light just a little while longer. Walk while you have the light, before darkness overtakes you. The man who walks in the dark does not know where he is going. Put your trust in the light while you have it, so that you may become sons of light'" (John 12:35, 36).

The prophets waited for Messiah, *Mashiach*, *Kristos*, the anointed one. Here are lineage prophecies that Jesus fulfilled: He would be a descendant of Isaac: "But my covenant I will establish with Isaac, whom Sarah will bear to you by this time next year" (Genesis 17:21). He would be from the tribe of Judah and from David through David's father Jesse: "A shoot will come up from the stump of Jesse; from his roots a Branch will bear fruit. The Spirit of the LORD will rest on him—" (Isaiah 11:1, 2).

God told David, "When your days are over and you rest with your fathers, I will raise up your offspring to succeed you, who will come from your own body, and I will establish his kingdom. He is the one who will build a house for my Name, and I will establish the throne of his kingdom forever. I will be his father, and he will be my son" (2 Samuel 7:12-14).

Jesus plainly said He was Messiah: "The woman at the well said, 'I know that Messiah' (called Christ) 'is coming. When he comes, he will explain everything to us.' Then Jesus declared, 'I who speak to you am he'" (John 4:25, 26). ". . . Again, the high priest asked him, 'Are you the Christ, the Son of the Blessed One?' 'I am,' said Jesus. 'And you will see the Son of Man sitting at the right hand of the Mighty One and coming on the clouds of heaven'" (Mark 14:61, 62).

Many Jewish people wait for the coming Messiah. But Jesus was the One to come. The prophecies He fulfilled are too many to be contrived or coincidental.

PRAY: *"Shine Your light into my inner mind, heart, and soul until no doubts remain."*

DAY 17 — DAYBREAK The Gate.

READING

"Enter through the narrow gate. For wide is the gate and broad is the road that leads to destruction, and many enter through it. But small is the gate and narrow the road that leads to life, and only a few find it" (Matthew 7:13, 14).

"Make every effort to enter through the narrow door, because many, I tell you, will try to enter and will not be able to" (Luke 13:24).

ENCOUNTER

Like the proverbial herd, the masses yearn to take the popular road. The wide road is the one easy to see, like flashing neon, attracting and sidetracking. Group psychology, majority rule, and social pressure influence the individual. Many rush through the wide gate only to fall over the cliff to certain destruction.

The sun shines lightly upon a small quiet lane. Only the fortunate find the way. It winds upward to the thin air of mountaintops to the narrow gate. There are no obvious markers but once you get through, the hosts of heaven will cheer your victorious entrance.

Jesus asks us to walk the narrow road, the high road, by following Him, though that way isn't fashionably correct or comfortable. He says repent, in Matthew 4:17: "From that time on Jesus began to preach, 'Repent, for the kingdom of heaven is near.'"

In Mark 10:21 He speaks of giving ourselves to Him entirely: " 'Go, sell everything you have and give to the poor, and you will have treasure in heaven. Then come, follow me.'"

He says deny yourself, in Matthew 16:24: ". . . If anyone would come after me, he must deny himself and take up his cross and follow me." He says give up your rights to yourself, "For whoever wants to save his life will lose it, but whoever loses his life for me will find it. What good will it be for a man if he gains the whole world, yet forfeits his soul? Or what can a man give in exchange for his soul?" (Matthew 16:25, 26).

He demands that we should be radical and disciplined. Am I prepared to give up everything for God? Am I ready to lose my life for His sake? What am I willing to do?

"So the last shall be first, and the first last; for many be called, but few chosen" (Matthew 20:16, KJV). Perhaps your time to take the high road has come. Choose which gate to enter! Some take the broad road and miss entering among the inner circle of "the elect."

When your time comes, treat the occasion as if it were once in a lifetime. The opportunity may only come once. Don't delay! Scripture says, ". . . Now is the time of God's favor, now is the day of salvation" (2 Corinthians 6:2).

PRAY: *"I can't find the way. It's too easy to take the highway to destruction and miss the lane to the narrow gate. Take my hand and lead me from my blindness into light."*

DAY 17 — SUNDOWN The Gate.

READING

". . . I am the gate for the sheep" (John 10:7).

"I am the gate; whoever enters through me will be saved. He will come in and go out, and find pasture" (John 10:9).

ENCOUNTER

It's generous to say that "all roads lead to heaven" whatever one's belief system. It's kinder to say, "Men of all creeds can live peaceably together and we all will make it to heaven, each in our own way." Or, put another way, "At least I believe in something." Yet, a theology that permits alternate salvation paths, though a popular belief is a lie.

Opening many doors onto heaven puts one in a maze of spiritual choices and obscures the one true door. Not only does the narrow gate lead to heaven, but also Jesus is the gate. Jesus said that all other ways to God but through Him are dead ends.

You may think this belief, without room for alternate views, is too restrictive. It sounds elitist, even ridiculous. But Christianity is exclusive because Truth is absolute. You may think, "I'm sincere in my own beliefs— that's what matters." Say you truly believe you're a great diver, so you take the leap from Niagara Falls. It's been done. Will that sincere belief pay off for you?

Only one door leads to heaven and Jesus Christ is that door. He said that He is the only way. The door is open and He asks us to enter. We can only enter by faith, willingly. Christianity offers, and delivers, a personal relationship with God.

In Frank Stockton's short story "The Lady or the Tiger," a prisoner must make a decision to go through one of two doors. Behind one door is the love of a lady and behind the other is a tiger and certain death. [7]

Like the prisoner, we too can choose the "door" to death or life. Jesus speaks of His loved ones as sheep and Himself as the Great Shepherd. "I am the good shepherd. The good shepherd lays down his life for the sheep" (John 10:11). "I am the good shepherd; I know my sheep and my sheep know me" (John 10:14).

Don't fear Him. Don't hate the One who gave Himself for humanity. Jesus said, ". . . I lay down my life for the sheep" (John 10:15).

Jesus also said, "Here I am! I stand at the door and knock. If anyone hears my voice and opens the door, I will come in and eat with him, and he with me" (Revelation 3:20).

Jesus is the entrance, the gate, and the door. Jesus opens the door a crack. He wants us to know Him. Swing the gate open. Don't perish with those of whom He says, in John 5:40, ". . . You refuse to come to me to have life." Enter through Jesus. Find Eternal Life.

PRAY: *"I hear Your knock. I hear Your soft voice calling me. The door is open and inviting, but I'm unsure and afraid. Come in, Jesus."*

DAY 18 — DAYBREAK The Way.

READING

". . . God our Savior, who wants all men to be saved and to come to knowledge of the truth. For there is one God and one mediator between God and men, the man Christ Jesus" (1 Timothy 2:3-5).

". . . God has given us eternal life, and this life is in his Son. He who has the Son has life; he who does not have the Son of God does not have life" (1 John 5:11, 12).

"No one who denies the Son has the Father; whoever acknowledges the Son has the Father also" (1 John 2:23).

ENCOUNTER

We might think we know God the Father. The time may come when Jesus draws us to Himself . . . then we'll truly know. And who is Jesus? A man? A prophet? Someone from another planet? Can you say that you know Jesus is the Son of God? Do you believe in the Son? Have you received Him? If I don't believe in the Son this way, then Scripture says I really don't have the Father or the Son.

We think we see but are blind. We think we live but without Eternal Life. We have either everlasting life or everlasting death. Eternal Life becomes ours by believing in the risen Son of God. He's there for us. We receive life through Jesus.

We can know the Son not as a historic theologian, but as the One who defeated death and is alive. A rich man asked Jesus, "Teacher, what good thing must I do to get eternal life?" (Matthew 19:16). Few of us would do what Jesus told him. "If you want to be perfect, go, sell your possessions and give to the poor, and you will have treasure in heaven. Then come, follow me" (Matthew 19:21).

If we know Jesus, then we have the Father too! Jesus is the way. You might say, "But I don't know the way!" See Acts 16:31: "Believe in the Lord Jesus, and you will be saved . . ." . You might say, "But, I don't know what to do!" "Believe in the Lord Jesus, and you will be saved." If we don't have both the Son and the Father, then we have neither.

Some would say that the Messiah is only for the Jewish people. That contradicts what God proclaimed through the Jewish prophet Isaiah. "It is too small a thing for you to be my servant to restore the tribes of Jacob and bring back those of Israel I have kept. I will also make you [Messiah] a light for the Gentiles, that you may bring my salvation to the ends of the earth" (Isaiah 49:6). See also Isaiah 52:13-15. It's no surprise that Messianic Jews, believers in Jesus, would embrace Gentiles that believe in Jesus. Jesus is the way to God for all peoples.

Know Him by believing. Have Him by receiving. God gives this gift to us. It's not enough to believe. We must receive Him in our hearts. "You believe that there is one God. Good! Even the demons believe that— and shudder" (James 2:19). Take Jesus now! He won't turn you away. Live forever. Find Eternal Life.

PRAY: *"God, show me the way—Your way!"*

DAY 18 — SUNDOWN The Way.

READING

"Whoever believes in the Son has eternal life, but whoever rejects the Son will not see life, for God's wrath remains on him" (John 3:36).

"Christ Jesus came into the world to save sinners" (1 Timothy 1:15).

"Now this is eternal life: that they may know you, the only true God, and Jesus Christ, whom you have sent" (John 17:3).

". . . I am the way and the truth and the life. No one comes to the Father except through me" (John 14:6).

ENCOUNTER

The claim "except through me," or except through JESUS, might sound outrageous, and even radical to the point of absurd. If you want to go to the Father, you must go through Jesus. So different from the "all paths lead to heaven" philosophy that's so prevalent.

Imagine that you're sitting in the defendant's chair. As you look around, the proportions of the courtroom are intimidating. And that's not all that's unsettling. The legal procedures are foreign to you and the questions posed by the prosecutor are difficult. In Franz Kafka's novel, The Trial, the innocent hero Josef K., is unexpectedly arrested one morning. Ultimately, the tribunal executes K. for reasons unknown.

To allay your fears, when you're in legal trouble, it makes sense to have an experienced attorney on your side. Your hope rests with the expert. He's able to defend you from the full wrath of the law. You may even be "somewhat" guilty—no matter. The lawyer is your advocate with the jury, pleading your innocence, or your mediator with the judge to bargain your sentence. The lawyer is your only way out. There's no way you can defend yourself.

As in a courtroom, God is the Judge of men, upholding the law. God knows that I'm guilty. Perhaps taking the position that we're born condemned also seems absurd, irrational, and undeserved as it did to Josef K. Remember, we're descendants of Adam and Eve, banished from the Garden. Yet, even as I'm found guilty, God is satisfied to lighten my sentence and proclaim me innocent. God's wrath is pacified because my lawyer, Jesus, is relentless to present me innocent. But who to punish? Jesus, though He's our lawyer, has already taken our guilt and the sentence of death upon Himself. He's been executed in our place. With Jesus as the go-between, we're exonerated and pardoned.

We're free! We're rescued because Jesus is our mediator, our Advocate with the Judge.

Jesus is the Way, the only way!

PRAY: *"I always thought I could know God directly. I see that I can only reach the Father through Jesus. It's hard to understand how finding Jesus has opened up the way that I always needed to find."*

DAY 19 — DAYBREAK The Sinless One.

READING

"Because he himself suffered when he was tempted, he is able to help those who are being tempted" (Hebrews 2:18).

". . . [Jesus] has been tempted in every way, just as we are— yet was without sin" (Hebrews 4:15).

ENCOUNTER

In Greek mythology, spellbinding singers called Sirens inhabited an island. Their alluring incantations seduced the minds of sailors, then drew them to shipwreck on the rocks. Odysseus wanted to be bound to the mast and have his sailor's ears plugged to escape these charmers.

Because I'm alive, I experience temptation. I might even feel powerless to resist. Temptation enchants us. It captivates, charms, and enraptures. Temptation enflames the passions. I can't escape by will alone.

When temptation comes to you, it always calls out your name.

"But each one is tempted when, by his own evil desire, he is dragged away and enticed. Then, after desire has conceived, it gives birth to sin; and sin, when it is full-grown, gives birth to death" (James 1:14, 15).

Supernatural forces, and our own desires, want to destroy and subject us to every indignity, to influence us into doing unholy acts. We can allow sin to overwhelm us, or with God's help, neutralize and overcome sin.

As a mortal, Jesus was tempted but He relied on His divine nature to endure. For forty days in the wilderness, He was enticed by Satan's promise of power, but He overcame. In the Garden of Gethsemane Jesus was haunted by the fear that He might run from the execution to which He had to submit. Jesus is the only person that never fell to temptation or sinned.

Jesus had to be innocent or He couldn't have fulfilled His purpose to atone for, and cleanse the human race. Shouldn't justice protect the blameless and punish the wrong? Christ as a substitute for the guilty was made sin, guilty, and wrong. "Christ redeemed us from the curse of the law by becoming a curse for us, for it is written: 'Cursed is everyone who is hung on a tree'" (Galatians 3:13). (See also Deuteronomy 21:22; 23.)

What meaning is there for a sinner to die for a sinner? But if a perfect man dies for a sinner . . . .

PRAY: *"Jesus, sinless One, what discipline You had— to live but never fall. Help me to understand how Your sinless life directly impacts me. How do I accept that, the penalty You received in my place substitutes for the punishment I deserve?"*

DAY 19 — SUNDOWN The Sinless One.

READING

"God made him who had no sin to be sin for us, so that in him we might become the righteousness of God" (2 Corinthians 5:21).

ENCOUNTER

Jesus was sinless. He became like us, so he could make us to become like Him.

In The Brothers Karamazov, Fyodor Dostoyevsky relates a fictional account of Christ's return and second arrest during the Spanish inquisition. "[The Grand Inquisitor] stretches forth his finger and orders the guard to take him . . . and lead him away. As one man the crowd immediately bows to the ground before the aged Inquisitor." [8]

Then the Grand Inquisitor says to Christ, ". . . you will see this obedient flock, which at my first gesture will rush to heap hot coals around your stake, at which I shall burn you for having come to interfere with us. For if anyone has ever deserved our stake, it is you." [9]

Dostoyevsky's tale symbolizes the events of Jesus' crucifixion. Jesus' crime wasn't deception. He was who He claimed to be. The spiritual leaders knew He was the promised one. The authorities in Jerusalem and those in Dostoyevsky's story didn't want to lose their power.

The Jewish law accused Jesus. The high priest had a distinguished legal mind. Yet, in the trial by night, Caiaphas broke laws that he was bound to observe. At Jesus' trial, witnesses contradicted themselves and gave accounts that didn't corroborate the accusation. The leaders were afraid that Jesus wanted their place and that Rome would destroy the temple. Because the innocent prisoner remained silent, He was condemned.

Though Jewish law accused Jesus, the Roman governor Pontius Pilate believed He was innocent. Pilate's wife had a dream that Jesus wasn't guilty. Pilate announced publicly, "I find no basis for a charge against this man" (Luke 23:4), and washed his hands to symbolize he wouldn't condemn a guiltless man. Yet, God allowed a Gentile punishment, crucifixion, for His Son.

What about the masses, His people? ". . . The chief priests and the elders persuaded the crowd . . ." (Matthew 27:20). Mob desire prevailed and they betrayed Him. Their lust for innocent blood was appeased. "Crucify Him! Crucify Him!" they shouted. They couldn't know what they were saying for He was innocent. It was the time of their visitation, their time to receive the Messiah, but they were blind. Jesus said of Himself, ". . . You did not recognize the time of God's coming to you" (Luke 19:44).

Jesus staggered under the burden of civilization, carrying the total sin of humanity. Blameless, Jesus was made leprosy for us lepers. He was made into our sin, and then punished for us. Therefore, we become God's righteousness and perfection. Allow Him to take your sins. Be washed clean.

PRAY: *"You, who are without sin, make me sinless, too!"*

DAY 20 — DAYBREAK The Crucifixion.

READING

". . . Knowing that all was now completed, and so that the Scripture would be fulfilled, Jesus said, 'I am thirsty.' A jar of wine vinegar was there, so they soaked a sponge in it, put the sponge on a stalk of the hyssop plant, and lifted it to Jesus' lips. When he had received the drink, Jesus said, 'It is finished.' With that, he bowed his head and gave up his spirit" (John 19:28-30).

". . . [Jesus] made himself nothing, taking the very nature of a servant, being made in human likeness. And being found in appearance as a man, he humbled himself and became obedient to death— even death on a cross!" (Philippians 2:7, 8).

ENCOUNTER

The worker of miracles who said He was the Son of God was in custody. It seemed all Jerusalem was out that day amid the roar and the crush. The masses enjoyed the exhibition, waiting for some spectacular sight. Would Jesus miraculously escape, overthrow His accusers, and take revenge?

Jesus, in the arena, was spent. He was the first "Christian" martyr, the Martyr of martyrs. Like an Olympian warrior, He was relentless, unswerving to his goal. He approached the finish with His body bruised and face pummeled. Time stopped as they lifted Him up.

The stark sign over the condemned's head stated His crime. Pontius Pilate commanded that the "*titulus*" must be written in Greek, Latin, and Hebrew. The entire charge against Jesus is assembled here from Matthew 27:37, Mark 15:26, Luke 23:38, and John 19:19.

"THIS IS JESUS THE NAZARENE, THE KING OF THE JEWS"

OYTOS	*ESTIN*	*IESUS*	*O*	*NAZORAIOS,*	*O BASILEUS*	*TON*	*IOUDAIOS*	[Greek]
HIC	*EST*	*IEUSUS*		*NAZARENUS,*	*REX*		*IUDAEORUM*	[Latin]
ZEH	*HU*	*YESHUA*		*NETZER,*	*MELEKH*	*HA*	*YAHUDIM*	[Hebrew]

The phony charge was that Jesus claimed to be a king. His crime was who He said He was; not any thing He did. It takes courage to be humiliated, and hurt especially if you can strike back but don't. Who killed Jesus? He said, "I lay down my life . . . No one takes it from me, but I lay it down of my own accord. I have authority to lay it down and . . . take it up again" (John 10:17, 18). Matthew 26:53 states that Jesus could call upon twelve legions (72,000) of angels to rescue Him. As a mortal, He feared death. Maybe He feared His human nature would stop Him from finishing the job. Instead, His divine nature faced down fear. No one's ever done a greater thing.

The burning sun parched Jesus entirely. Christ, wounded in battle, cried out for water from an immense thirst, aggravated by distress, loss of blood, and intense fever from inflamed injuries.

Jesus, "The Water of Life," was drained by the fires of hell. The hot, bitter fight, the contest severe, He gave in to death— the cost to overcome death in victory was by His own death! The "King of Kings" died! Passive? Defeated? No! He achieved a totally successful conquest. ". . . Having disarmed the powers and authorities, he made a public spectacle of them, triumphing over them by the cross" (Colossians 2:15). He said, "It is finished," meaning, "My task is accomplished."

PRAY: *"King Jesus . . . How vital a thing You did for me, and for all people."*

DAY 20 — SUNDOWN The Crucifixion.

READING

"One of the criminals who hung there hurled insults at him: 'Aren't you the Christ? Save yourself and us!' But the other criminal rebuked him. 'Don't you fear God,' he said, 'since you are under the same sentence? We are punished justly, for we are getting what our deeds deserve. But this man has done nothing wrong.' Then he said, 'Jesus, remember me when you come into your kingdom.' Jesus answered him, 'I tell you the truth, today you will be with me in paradise'" (Luke 23:39-43).

ENCOUNTER

The seven recorded utterances by Jesus from the cross in presumed order are as follows:

"Father, forgive them, for they do not know what they are doing."	Luke 23:33,34
"Today you will be with me in paradise."	Luke 23:43
"Woman, here is your son . . . Here is your mother!"	John 19:26,27
"My God, my God, why have you forsaken me?"	Matt. 27:45-47, Mark 15:34
"I am thirsty."	John 19:28
"It is finished."	John 19:30
"Father, into your hands I commit my spirit."	Luke 23:46

In crucifixion, the body is soaked with sweat and thirst is intense. The pain and shock are unbearable. Jesus suffered His agony, His passion, for humanity. Hanging by the arms, the sagging body drops into a spasm that prevents exhalation. The feet are nailed through the heel bone, a cruel "step" for support, so the victim can breathe.

Jesus was crucified naked and between two thieves. The three looked down upon the distorted scene, the noise and press of the crowd. The two with Jesus were desperate, as Jesus was the only one who could stay their execution and His own, but He wouldn't. The officials broke the thieves' legs, to speed their deaths, so the Passover wouldn't be defiled.

The first criminal's hard heart doomed him. The other repented, believed, and was saved in his final moments. We don't know the extent of his crime. He could have had the heart of a Stalin or Hitler. We do know he was condemned to die by the most horrible way of the Roman Empire. Suddenly, the thief believes in God, that Jesus is God and has a kingdom. He asks to join Jesus' kingdom. Jesus accepts him unconditionally, in the man's last moments, no matter what he did! Forgiveness is available . . . no matter what we've done. Jesus died for imperfect me.

Ignoring human instincts, Jesus had the courage to die, and the compassion to die for others. By His death, He beat our enemies, sin, death, and the devil. The triumph seems inverted by the world's standard. But the hero died while defeating the enemy, and then returned from the dead. "By his death he might destroy him who holds the power of death—that is, the devil—and free those who all their lives were held in slavery by their fear of death" (Hebrews 2:14, 15).

The two criminals symbolize two opposite types of humans. One goes to Eternal Life in paradise by his faith in Jesus' absolute forgiveness. The other chooses Eternal Life in hell. How do I choose to spend Eternal Life?

PRAY: *"Jesus, Lord, I recognize the sacrifice You made for me!"*

DAY 21 — DAYBREAK Crucifixion Miracles.

READING

". . . The sixth hour [noon], and darkness came over the whole land until the ninth hour [3 p.m.], for the sun stopped shining. And the curtain of the temple was torn in two. Jesus called out with a loud voice, 'Father, into your hands I commit My spirit.' When He had said this, He breathed His last" (Luke 23:44-46).

ENCOUNTER

Jesus had been shamefully suspended since nine that morning. During His ordeal, Christ received all four types of skin wounds: Abrasions to His scalp by the crown of thorns. Punctures to His wrists and feet by the nails. Lacerations to His body from scourging. An incision by the spear in His side.

Peter said of Jesus, "But this is how God fulfilled what he had foretold through all the prophets, saying that his Christ would suffer" (Acts 3:18).

At noon darkness from a solar eclipse crept in. All the while, the wind sounded like a howling wolf, like snapping canvas in a storm. The sun couldn't pierce the massive clouds as the black sky whorled above Calvary, "the place of the Skull." In a future day, the whole earth will dim before Jesus returns.

Jesus was crushed in the jaws of death's skull. The Bible depicts stillness and conclusion, an after-silence like an abating storm, as His breath fled from His collapsing lungs. The sun returned and somehow the birds chirped again.

"I hate you O Death, never sated, Your hungry wail in the night.

You cut down boys, wise men, grandmothers,

Young mothers and maidens. You strip us of dignity in our last moments."

Just as God commanded of Moses, the veil in the Hebrew temple that separated men from the Holy of Holies was suspended from four pillars of acacia wood overlaid with gold and held by gold hooks through silver sockets. The moment Jesus died, a tearing, ripping sound shattered the silence of the inner temple. Matthew 27:51 describes how God's finger sliced the thick linen curtain, twined of fine blue, purple, and scarlet, from top to bottom. If anyone dared, they could see through the torn partition and beyond the haze of incense to where the forbidden Ark of the Covenant rested, entirely overlaid in gold.

That spot, named "The Holiest of All," was exposed for the first time. Before Jesus' crucifixion, only priests could enter "The Most Holy Place," by the sprinkling of blood sacrifice. After Jesus' sacrifice it would no longer be God's requirement to sacrifice in the inner sanctuary because Jesus died, "once for all" (1 Peter 3:18). Christ opened the way for man into God's presence. "He broke down the partition between us" (Ephesians 2:14).

" . . . Enter into the holiest by the blood of Jesus, By a new and living way, which he hath consecrated for us, through the veil, that is to say, his flesh" (Hebrews 10:19-22).

PRAY: *"God, You prepared a better way for me to come into Your presence, to come before Your throne. I, a sinful man, am now permitted to pray to a Holy God."*

DAY 21 — SUNDOWN Crucifixion Miracles.

READING

"And at the ninth hour Jesus cried in a loud voice, 'Eloi, Eloi, lama sabachthani?'— which means, "My God, my God, why have you forsaken me?" "With a loud cry, Jesus breathed his last" (Mark 15:34, 37).

". . . The earth shook and the rocks split. The tombs broke open and the bodies of many holy people who had died were raised to life. They came out of the tombs, and after Jesus' resurrection, they went into the holy city and appeared to many people. When the centurion and those with him who were guarding Jesus saw the earthquake and all that had happened, they were terrified, and exclaimed, 'Surely he was the Son of God!'" (Matthew 27:51-54).

ENCOUNTER

With Jesus' last cry, vicious vibrations were triggered at a frequency that split rock. Burial caves crumbled, graves sank, and tombs tore open from the ground tremors.

The raw scene at the crucifixion and its aftermath created great fear in Jerusalem as many knew that God's Son was killed. The Roman centurion and the hundred soldiers under his command were terrified at the black sky and the ground bolting out of control.

People will do anything to stall death, to cheat it a while. Much is written about clinically dead people who return to life. They tell similar stories about places and persons seen while unconscious. They see themselves dead, they go through a tunnel, and they see a light.

After Christ died and resurrected, Matthew says many people witnessed known dead, holy people, miraculously raised to life. They walked outside the city and later entered Jerusalem. The exhumed citizens emphasize the everlasting victory over death by Christ's Resurrection. The miracles that occurred after Christ's death confirmed His deity.

After Rome killed Jesus, a miracle occurred in Jesus' small band of followers. They continued His cause spreading the news that Jesus is the Messiah, the Son of God. Why would they bother if Jesus were a failure? They were convinced that He rose from death and they would die for that truth. Christianity overcame all odds to become the world's great faith because its leader rose from the dead and He continues to direct His people.

The Gospels say that Jesus predicted His own death and Resurrection. Jesus said of Himself, ". . . The Son of man is delivered into the hands of men, and they shall kill him; and after he is killed, he shall rise the third day" (Mark 9:31).

Though Jesus tried to prepare His followers, they were despondent after His death and they scattered. Two days would quickly pass from Good Friday to Easter.

PRAY: *"Dear God, life after death is unthinkably precious. Will You make eternal life mine?"*

DAY 22 — DAYBREAK The Resurrection.

READING

". . . Why do you look for the living among the dead? He is not here; he has risen! Remember how he told you . . . 'The Son of Man must be delivered into the hands of sinful men, be crucified and on the third day be raised again'" (Luke 24:5-7).

ENCOUNTER

Good Friday's storm passed and then came Resurrection Sunday, the key event of history. Some disciples came to the tomb to express their grief, bringing ointment and spices for the corpse. But Jesus' body was gone! Who stole His body, and where was it taken? Here are some arguments of how the body disappeared:

Joseph of Arimathea and Nicodemus. They reclaimed the costly tomb by moving the body to another burial place. If so, who rolled the stone away from the guarded tomb?

The Roman authorities or guards. But for what purpose? The agitator was dead, forgotten. The body lay in a sealed tomb. Further, the guards could be killed for losing Him and leaving their post. Besides, the Jewish leaders set up their own watch to prevent the body from being stolen. They had most to lose if Israel believed Jesus rose from the dead. They knew He died, and that a miracle had occurred. Scripture documents that they bribed the soldiers to keep the Resurrection quiet (Matthew 28:12).

Jesus didn't die. He revived instead of resurrected and then walked away. Even if He were buried alive, how could He get out of the tomb? Scripture shows Jesus was pierced through the heart and died. "But, one of the soldiers, with a spear, pierced his side, and immediately came there out blood and water. The man who saw it has given testimony . . . He knows that he tells the truth, and he testifies so that you also may believe" (John 19:34, 35). Later, Jesus appeared in a spiritual, resurrected body, not of flesh, and was able to appear and disappear.

The wrong tomb. If so, the leaders could go to the correct tomb and produce the body.

Jesus' followers moved Him. They were frightened and in hiding. Even if they stole His dead body, Christianity would be based on a lie. Without the Resurrection, Christianity would have died in the first century. If His followers were wrong, then Christians are to be pitied and the world has no hope. "For if the dead are not raised, then Christ has not been raised either. And if Christ has not been raised, your faith is futile; you are still in your sins. If only for this life we have hope in Christ, we are to be pitied more than all men" (1 Corinthians 15:16 - 19).

If you seek an event to place your faith, the Resurrection explains two dilemmas: the enormous boulder rolled away, and the empty tomb. The Resurrection would not hold up If the tomb still held Jesus' body. Scripture says, the stone moved by an ". . . earthquake; for an angel of the Lord came down from heaven and . . . rolled back the stone and sat on it" (Matthew 28:2).

(Note: Who Moved the Stone by Frank Morison [10] and More Than a Carpenter by Josh McDowell [11] inspired the above narrative in part.)

PRAY: *"Help me to see that the only reason for the empty tomb was Jesus' Resurrection."*

DAY 22 — SUNDOWN The Resurrection.

READING

". . . His incomparably great power for us who believe. That power is like the working of His mighty strength, which he exerted in Christ when he raised him from the dead and seated him at his right hand in the heavenly realms . . ." (Ephesians 1:19, 20).

ENCOUNTER

"Joseph took the body, wrapped it in a clean linen cloth" (Matthew 27:59). The body lay at rest in Joseph's tomb. That first Easter Sunday, Jesus' Father exercised power as a brilliant flash, a force, raced through Jesus' grave clothes and out the hewn rock mausoleum. Christ was transformed; He was raised. No longer flesh, blood, and bones, He stood immortal, dignified, in a resurrected body. Jesus left his grave clothes intact, unwrapped, on the stone slab. He walked out of His wrappings and simply left the tomb.

After the Resurrection, ". . . [Peter] saw the strips of linen lying there, as well as the burial cloth that had been around Jesus' head. The cloth was folded up by itself, separate from the linen" (John 20:6, 7). Many believe the Shroud of Turin in Italy is the very burial cloth used to wrap Christ. The carbon dating of the shroud shows it's from the first century. A negative image of a crucified man, anatomically correct, and of Jesus' age, appears only on the front of the shroud. The wounds to the head and body, the Roman whip marks, and the bloodstains on the cloth are consistent with Christ's passion. Many pollen seeds and flowers, whose images are on the cloth, are found only near Jerusalem. Science can't resolve how the image was made. It wasn't dyed onto the fabric. If it is Christ's shroud, the image was made by Resurrection energy.

The Jewish historian Josephus wrote this extrabiblical account of the Resurrection: "Now, there was about this time, Jesus, a wise man; if it be lawful to call him a man, for he was a doer of wonderful works— a teacher of such men as receive the truth with pleasure. He drew over to him both many of the Jews, and many of the Gentiles. He was [the] Christ; and when Pilate, at the suggestion of the principal men amongst us, had condemned him to the cross, those that loved him at the first did not forsake him, for he appeared to them alive again the third day, as the divine prophets had foretold these and ten thousand other wonderful things concerning him; and the tribe of Christians, so named from him, are not extinct at this day." [12]

Peter wrote, in Acts 10:39-41, "We are witnesses of everything he did . . . They killed him by hanging him on a tree, but God raised him from the dead on the third day . . . He was not seen by all the people, but by witnesses whom God had already chosen— by us who ate and drank with him after he rose from the dead."

Jesus appeared alive after His Resurrection. What other spiritual leader, of any faith, rose from the dead and now lives? Only One, with whom you can speak in prayer. Because Jesus rose from the dead, His followers also will rise after death. ". . . I am the resurrection and the life. He who believes in me will live, even though he dies; and whoever lives and believes in me will never die. Do you believe this?" (John 11:25). "Because I live, you also will live" (John 14:19). "Christ was raised from the dead through the glory of the Father, we too may live a new life" (Romans 6:4).

PRAY: *"Jesus, You did it! You rose from the dead. At last, evidence that requires me to consider believing in You."*

DAY 23 — DAYBREAK Post-Resurrection Appearances.

READING

"'Woman,' He said, 'why are you crying? Who is it you are looking for?' Thinking he was the gardener, she said, 'Sir, if you have carried Him away, tell me where you have put him, and I will get him.' Jesus said to her, 'Mary.' She turned toward Him and cried out in Aramaic, 'Rabboni!' (Which means Teacher). Jesus said, 'Do not hold on to me, for I have not yet returned to the Father . . .'" (John 20:15-17).

ENCOUNTER

Mary and Jesus had said their good-byes in Emmaus. Now, with Him buried, she ached, believing she'd never see Him again. She missed His voice, walk, expressions, the events they shared, their nonverbal understandings. She felt the hard edge of loss; her grief burdened her like a weight. Tears stung her blurred eyes.

The most intimate word Jesus will ever say to a person is her name. When God speaks, the moment is a sacred experience. The young woman from Magdala heard the tender speech of her Lord when He called to her by the tomb. Maybe she held in her breath when He called her name. Then, she saw Him. She tried to hug Him for they were as siblings reunited. She ran to tell the disciples He came back from death . . . but they didn't believe her!

"Then some of our companions went to the tomb and found it just as the women had said, but him they did not see.' He said to them, 'How foolish you are, and how slow of heart to believe all that the prophets have spoken! Did not the Christ have to suffer these things and then enter his glory? And beginning with Moses and all the Prophets, he explained to them what was said in all the Scriptures concerning himself'" (Luke 24:24-27).

What kind of woman was Mary? Like Jesus, she was from the north. Her village, Magdala, was near the Sea of Galilee. We know she was grateful, for Jesus freed her from adultery, prostitution, and spiritual bondage. Luke 8:2 records that Jesus cast seven demons out of her. She was forgiven much, so she felt she owed much. Having known men, she was worldly before her time, though young and probably insecure. Perhaps her nails were close-bitten, the bright paint chipping. She had an earthy look about her. A downcast stance and her quick nervous movements reflected the indignities and persecution of her lifestyle.

Perhaps because of low self-esteem Mary felt unworthy to stand closer to the cross. Luke 23:49 says that when He was crucified, she and others "stood at a distance, watching these things." Yet, she was one of only a few followers who were courageous enough to view the crucifixion. Jesus honored her courage by letting her be the first to witness His return from the dead. The transformation of the other disciples from cowards to bold witnesses is evidence that Christ also appeared to them after His Resurrection.

". . . Christ died for our sins . . . he was buried . . . raised on the third day according to the Scriptures . . . appeared to Peter and then to the Twelve. After that, he appeared to more than five hundred of the brothers at the same time . . . Then he appeared to James, then to all the apostles, and last of all he appeared to me [Paul] also" (1 Corinthians 15:3-8).

PRAY: *"I need to hear my name spoken by You, my Creator."*

DAY 23 — SUNDOWN Post-Resurrection Appearances.

READING

". . . When the disciples were together, with the doors locked for fear of the Jews, Jesus came and stood among them and said, 'Peace be with you!'" (John 20:19).

ENCOUNTER

The evening of the Resurrection, the disciples met secretly. Their leader was buried. They were afraid, discouraged, and broken-hearted. They couldn't grasp why he died. They hadn't understood that the Resurrection was a sign. ". . . What miraculous sign can you show us to prove your authority to do all this?' Jesus answered them, 'Destroy this temple, and I will raise it again in three days'" (John 2:18, 19). He referred to the temple of His body.

The Messiah is to be a deliverer, like Moses, as written in Deuteronomy 18:15. The disciples expected Him to defeat the Romans, and set up a Messianic kingdom. They were so disappointed when He was taken that they abandoned Him to be crucified.

Suddenly, He appeared in His immortal body, from nowhere, through walls. Time or matter doesn't bind Jesus. His resurrected body looked something like flesh and bones. The disciples were afraid, thinking He was a spirit. Thomas put his finger to the nail prints in Christ's wrists and lance-speared side to be sure it was He. He wished them *Shalom*, Peace. Jesus offers peace in life's storms and courage for our struggles.

Days later, in Galilee, Jesus cooked fish over hot coals and asked Peter to eat. To show forgiveness, three times He asked Peter of his love, for each of Peter's denials. After Jesus rose, Cleopas and another traveler had dinner with Him in the Emmaus inn. Once they recognized Him, He disappeared. He could appear or disappear at will. His Resurrection shows that, after death, our bodies also will be of a spiritual essence that will work differently than our physical bodies.

What did He say to them after His Resurrection? Luke said, ". . . I wrote about all that Jesus began to do and to teach until the day he was taken up to heaven after giving instructions through the Holy Spirit to the apostles he had chosen. After his suffering, he showed himself to these men and gave many convincing proofs that he was alive. He appeared to them over a period of forty days and spoke about the kingdom of God" (Acts 1:1-3). He validated the Bible by quoting Scripture. He read the Bible to them until they understood. He showed how He fulfilled prophecy. He said, "Tell others about Me."

How can you explain that frightened, sequestered disciples became inspired, outspoken, and ultimately enabled with supernatural power sent from above?

The answer is that Jesus arose from the dead. He appeared to His disciples and no power on earth could prevent them from proclaiming the truth that they knew firsthand. More than five hundred people believed that they saw Jesus after He was resurrected.

Not everyone is willing to die for the truth, but no one is willing to die for a lie. All of the original twelve disciples, except John, died a violent death for their beliefs in Jesus.

PRAY: *"Appear to me in some miraculous way. Change me forever by Your power."*

DAY 24 — DAYBREAK The Resurrection of Believers.

READING

"And the dust return to the ground it came from, and the spirit returns to God who gave it" (Ecclesiastes 12:7).

"But your dead will live; their bodies will rise. You who dwell in the dust, wake up and shout for joy. Your dew is like the dew of the morning; the earth will give birth to her dead" (Isaiah 26:19).

"Multitudes who sleep in the dust of the earth will awake: some to everlasting life, others to shame and everlasting contempt" (Daniel 12:2, 3).

". . . You will be repaid at the resurrection of the righteous" (Luke 14:14).

". . . A time is coming when all who are in their graves will hear his voice" (John 5:28).

"What you sow does not come to life unless it dies . . ." (1 Corinthians 15:36).

". . . The resurrection of the dead. The body that is sown is perishable, it is raised imperishable; it is sown in dishonor, it is raised in glory; it is sown in weakness, it is raised in power; it is sown a natural body, it is raised a spiritual body . . ." (1 Corinthians 15:42-44).

". . . The one who raised the Lord Jesus from the dead will also raise us with Jesus" (2 Corinthians 4:14).

". . . To be absent from the body, and to be present with the Lord" (2 Corinthians 5:8, KJV).

"For we must all appear before the judgment seat of Christ, that each one may receive what is due him for the things done while in the body . . ." (2 Corinthians 5:10).

". . . Receive a rich welcome into the eternal kingdom of our Lord and Savior Jesus Christ" (2 Peter 1:11).

"I saw the dead, small and great, stand before God . . ." (Revelation 20:12, 13, KJV).

ENCOUNTER

Our destiny is to be raised after we die. The death of the body is inevitable, and so too is the eternity of our spirit. We live forever! The time we spend in the grave, unconscious, will pass in an instant. We'll waken from death, in God's presence, as from a nap, though we may have lain there thousands of years.

Behind the eye sockets, inside our clay body, is an eternal being waiting to be freed from the bonds of time and space. We waste so much time trying to beautify our face and bodies. We're as butterflies suspended in a chrysalis. My spirit yearns for freedom. There's life after death . . . Eternal Life.

PRAY: *"I want to live . . . forever."*

DAY 24 — SUNDOWN The Resurrection of Believers.

READING

". . . A time is coming and has now come when the dead will hear the voice of the Son of God and those who hear will live" (John 5:25).

". . . What we will be has not yet been made known. But we know that when he appears, we shall be like him, for we shall see him as he is" (1 John 3:2).

". . . Transform our lowly bodies so that they will be like his glorious body" (Philippians 3:21).

". . . So shall we bear the likeness of the man from heaven . . . flesh and blood cannot inherit the kingdom of God . . . I tell you a mystery: We will not all sleep, but we will all be changed—in a flash, in the twinkling of an eye, at the last trumpet. For the trumpet will sound, the dead will be raised imperishable . . ." (1 Corinthians 15:49-52).

"When Christ, who is your life, appears, then you also will appear with him in glory" (Colossians 3:4).

ENCOUNTER

No one has seen God the Father exactly as He is, though a few have seen a reflection of His likeness. Mortals perish before God's glory. Someday our immortal bodies will be like His. We'll know Him face to face.

The Old Covenant prophet Isaiah had a vision: "I saw the Lord seated on a throne, high and exalted, and the train of his robe filled the temple. Above him were seraphs . . . they were calling to one another: 'Holy, holy, holy is the LORD Almighty; the whole earth is full of his glory'" (Isaiah 6:1-3).

Another Old Covenant prophet, Ezekiel was also privileged to see God. "I saw that from what appeared to be his waist up he looked like glowing metal, as if full of fire . . . brilliant light surrounded him. Like the appearance of a rainbow in the clouds on a rainy day . . . the appearance of the likeness of the glory of the LORD . . . I fell facedown . . ." (Ezekiel 1:27, 28).

". . . As Christ was raised from the dead through the glory of the Father, we too may live a new life. If we have been united with him like this in his death, we will certainly also be united with him in his resurrection" (Romans 6:4, 5).

"And if the Spirit of him who raised Jesus from the dead is living in you, he who raised Christ from the dead will also give life to your mortal bodies through his Spirit, who lives in you" (Romans 8:11). Jesus rose, and because He did, His followers too, will rise to Eternal Life.

"Twilight and evening Bell, And after that the dark! And may there be no sadness of farewell, When I embark; For though from out our bourne of time and place, The flood may bear me far, I hope to see my pilot face to face, When I have crossed the bar." [13]

PRAY: *"I want to see You Lord, high and lifted up in Your immortality, and be like You."*

DAY 25 — DAYBREAK The Ascension.

READING

"When he had led them out to the vicinity of Bethany, he lifted up his hands . . . While he was blessing them he was taken up into heaven. Then they worshipped him and returned to Jerusalem with great joy. And they stayed continually at the temple, praising God" (Luke 24:50-53).

ENCOUNTER

Recall the sweet story, recorded in John 20, of Mary Magdalene who visited Jesus' tomb not knowing He'd risen from the dead. He told her, ". . . Do not hold on to me, for I have not yet returned to the Father. Go instead to my brothers and tell them, 'I am returning to my Father and your Father, to my God and your God.'" Jesus was referring to His ascension to heaven.

In the bullring, there's a spot the Spanish call *la querencia*, or home ground, the favorite place of comfort the doomed bull selects. It's the corner where he continues to return. How natural that the village of Bethany was Jesus' last stop before the crucifixion <u>and</u> His final stop before His ascension! Bethany was the home of Jesus' friends, Mary, Martha, and Lazarus.

Jesus delivered His last blessing while He rose, even as God spoke from heaven. The words caused the disciples to worship and praise God with joy that glowed for days. Lifting his hands, Jesus' rising body arced toward heaven. How does a King ascend bodily with dignity? Did He rise slowly? Did angels surround Him? Did His image remain the same size as He receded upward until the portals of God's kingdom opened, and He vanished? Heaven's choir sang unceasingly, "Holy, Holy, Holy" in unison, like a harmonized aria . . . the scene, a Renaissance painter's delight. Heaven welcomed the Conqueror and "all hailed King Jesus" as He took His place by the Father's right side.

Jesus' last words are written in Luke 24:49: "I am going to send you what my Father has promised; but stay in the city until you have been clothed with power from on high." Jesus was referring to God's promise of the Holy Spirit who would come. In Joel 2:28 we read, "And afterward, I will pour out my Spirit on all people . . .". Joel's prophecy was fulfilled, as recorded in Acts 1:8, "But you will receive power when the Holy Spirit comes on you." (More on spiritual birth and the Holy Spirit later.)

When the disciple Stephen was martyred, he saw Jesus standing in heaven. "But Stephen, full of the Holy Spirit, looked up to heaven and saw the glory of God, and Jesus standing at the right hand of God" (Acts 7:55).

Paul speaks of the future translation of Christians in the air, what's called the Rapture. ". . . We do not want you to be ignorant about those who fall asleep, or to grieve like the rest of men, who have no hope. We believe that Jesus died and rose again and so we believe that God will bring with Jesus those who have fallen asleep in him. According to the Lord's own word . . . we who are still alive, who are left till the coming of the Lord, will certainly not precede those who have fallen asleep. For the Lord himself will come down from heaven . . . the dead in Christ will rise first. After that, we who are still alive and are left will be caught up together with them in the clouds to meet the Lord in the air. And so we will be with the Lord forever" (1 Thessalonians 4:13 – 17).

PRAY: *"To have been there to see Your rapturous glory in ascension and to hear Your blessing!"*

DAY 25 — SUNDOWN The Ascension.

READING

". . . He was taken up before their very eyes, and a cloud hid him from their sight. They were looking intently up into the sky as he was going, when suddenly two men dressed in white stood beside them. 'Men of Galilee,' they said, 'why do you stand here looking into the sky? This same Jesus, who has been taken from you into heaven, will come back in the same way you have seen him go into heaven. Then they returned to Jerusalem from the hill called the Mount of Olives . . .'" (Acts 1:9-12).

ENCOUNTER

It's another world at 30,000 feet. The sky is a gradient of aqua to deep navy, then black beyond the thin atmosphere to the cosmos. Below is the cloud foundation, a sterile carpet of thick fingers, dense tufts of an unbroken ridge. Six-sided ice crystals multiply into monolithic monuments of snow. The deafening sound of gale force winds blocks the din of the world, with its troubles and pain.

As Christ pierced the deck of clouds, He was hidden as He passed to the heavens. He returned to the place men and women of all the ages have desired to see and yearned for wings to fly. Some Roman emperors and certain prophets allegedly ascended to heaven as their followers claimed, but none of those men ever said they were the Son of God.

I recall the excitement and sadness of being a passenger on an ocean liner. We were thrilled to be on a voyage, yet as we slowly pulled out of port, we saw my family waving to us from the pier, many, regrettably, for the last time. We learned later that they stayed until the boat vanished, longing to go with us on the trip but having to return to their routine lives. Like my family, the disciples stared up long after the vision of Christ dissolved. Jesus entered heaven to sit at "the right hand of God" (Mark 16:19), waiting for the fullness of time to permit His return.

From heaven, Jesus knows how to pray for His people, having lived on earth. ". . . He had to be made like his brothers in every way, in order that he might become a merciful and faithful high priest in service to God, and that he might make atonement for the sins of the people. Because he himself suffered when he was tempted, he is able to help those who are being tempted" (Hebrews 2:17, 18). And God's Son can cleanse the sins of every person ever born.

The two "men" in white hinted that He would return. Will I know when Messiah comes, that He is Jesus? Yes, because He will return in the clouds. Revelation 1:7 says, "Look, he is coming with the clouds, and every eye will see him . . .". Before Jesus returns bodily, many false prophets will claim they are He and some will be empowered by Satan to deceive the world.

Peter said of Jesus, "He must remain in heaven until the time comes for God to restore everything, as he promised long ago through his holy prophets" (Acts 3:21).

Jesus will return to earth as He predicted. He will come visibly in the eastern sky and descend to the Mount of Olives from where He ascended. "On that day his feet will stand on the Mount of Olives, east of Jerusalem . . ." (Zechariah 14:4).

PRAY: *"I want to see You by sight and by Spirit. Until the day we meet, Amen."*

DAY 26 — DAYBREAK The Visual Return.

READING

". . . False Christs and false prophets will appear and perform great signs and miracles . . . if anyone tells you, 'There he is, out in the desert,' do not go out; or, 'Here he is, in the inner rooms,' do not believe it. For as lightning that comes from the east is visible even in the west, so will be the coming of the Son of Man" (Matthew 24:24-27).

ENCOUNTER

The time approaches like a long night that will dawn to witness Jesus' return from His ascendancy. Christians wait for His return event even as the season before Christmas, for it will usher in eternal Christmas. These events, predicted in the Bible thousands of years ago, have already occurred:

1930-40s. The Holocaust—the genocide of the Jewish people in Europe in World War II. The valley full of dry bones is Israel about to be reborn (Ezekiel 37:1-3).

1945. The fall of Germany. The Holocaust ends. Where was God when six million Jewish people were killed during WWII? Yet God preserved them during centuries of dispersion, and then brought Israel to life. ". . . The Sovereign LORD says to these bones: I will make breath enter you, and you will come to life. I will attach tendons to you and make flesh come upon you and cover you with skin . . . Then you will know that I am the LORD . . . O my people, I am going to open your graves and bring you up from them; I will bring you back to the land of Israel" (Ezekiel 37:5, 6, 12).

1948. The birth of the modern State of Israel as the earth's clock began winding down for the end times and for Messiah's return. "I will bring back my exiled people Israel . . . never again to be uprooted" (Amos 9:14, 15). ". . . In the latter years thou shalt come into the land that is brought back from the sword, and is gathered out of many people, against the mountains of Israel, which have been always waste . . . they shall dwell safely, all of them" (Ezekiel 38:8, KJV). "In days to come Jacob will take root, Israel will bud and blossom and fill all the world with fruit" (Isaiah 27:6). In Luke 21:29, the parable of the fig tree (symbolic of Israel) that blooms describes Israel's rebirth.

1967. The Six-Day War ends; the unification of Jerusalem under Jewish rule. "Jerusalem will be trampled on by the Gentiles until the times of the Gentiles are fulfilled" (Luke 21:24).

1973. The Yom Kippur War. Israel's borders were miraculously protected. ". . . Jerusalem will be a city without walls because of the great number of men and livestock in it. 'And I myself will be a wall of fire around it . . . I will be its glory within'" (Zechariah 2:4, 5).

1993. The alliance between Israel and the Vatican predicted in Revelation 17:9 and Daniel 7:7 by the signing of the "Fundamental Agreement between the Holy See and the State of Israel" that recognized Israel. The "seven heads" some believe to be seven Caesars and the seven hills of Rome, the mountain on which the woman sits. In Revelation 17:18, the woman is the great city that reigns over the kings of the earth. The ten horns are ten kings of the end times Rome.

Christians in each generation think their time to be the last days. Since Jesus' ascension, His return has been approaching. Since the rebirth of Israel in 1948, His return is imminent.

PRAY: *"God, thank You for Your timetable of world events, and for revealing to us the future."*

DAY 26 — SUNDOWN The Visual Return.

READING

"What will be the sign of your coming and of the end of the age?" (Matthew 24:3, 4).

ENCOUNTER

The disciples asked Christ to name the last generation. "When are You coming back? When's the end of time?" Jesus answers, in Luke 17:26, 27, "Just as it was in the days of Noah, so also will it be in the days of the Son of Man. People were eating, drinking, marrying and being given in marriage up to the day Noah entered the ark. Then the flood came and destroyed them all."

Jesus will return suddenly and quickly, like in childbirth. "While people are saying, 'Peace and safety,' destruction will come on them suddenly, as labor pains on a pregnant woman, and they will not escape" (1 Thessalonians 5:3). Christ will return visibly, like a thunderbolt in the clouds, "For as lightning that comes from the east is visible even in the west, so will be the coming of the Son of Man" (Matthew 24:27).

In Noah's day, God, sorry that He made man and all life, wanted to destroy the earth. Near the end of the world, it will be like in the days of Noah, described in Genesis 6:4-7 and Genesis 6:11-13. Wickedness will be great. Imagination, thoughts, motives, purposes, and desires will be evil, corrupt, and violent.

Jesus continued answering questions about the last days in Luke 17:28, 29: "It was the same in the days of Lot. People were eating and drinking, buying and selling, planting and building. But the day Lot left Sodom, fire and sulfur rained down from heaven and destroyed them all." The men of Sodom were homosexual. Shamelessly perverse, they sought sex even with the angels (Genesis 18:20-23; 19:4, 5).

Christ's return will be like Lot's days as recalled in 2 Peter 2:6-10. The cry of Sodom and Gomorrah was great, like the cry of righteous Abel's blood, murdered by Cain. The Bible predicts that at the end, our sin, like Sodom, will be grievous, wicked, ungodly, filthy, unlawful, unjust, lustful, hating authority, anarchistic, self-willed, blasphemous, and despising dignities.

As morality declines, the world, not expecting a cataclysm, will carry on as usual. ". . . The day of the Lord will come like a thief in the night" (1 Thessalonians 5:2). The day will come without warning— we won't know when. Suddenly the flood came and destroyed them. Fire and brimstone rained from heaven upon Sodom and Gomorrah. Luke 17:30 says, "Even thus shall it be in the day when the Son of man is revealed."

At the end times, also called "The Day of the Lord," "The heavens will disappear with a roar; the elements will be destroyed by fire, and the earth and everything in it will be laid bare" (2 Peter 3:10). "For the Son of Man will come in his Father's glory with his angels, and then he will reward each person according to what he has done . . . some who are standing here will not taste death before they see the Son of Man coming in his kingdom" (Matthew 16:27, 28).

PRAY: *"Dear God, the signs are frightening. I'm convicted by the ancient writings that describe our modern world."*

DAY 27 — DAYBREAK The Spiritual Birth.

READING

"And afterward, I will pour out my Spirit on all people. Your sons and daughters will prophesy, your old men will dream dreams, your young men will see visions" (Joel 2:28, 29).

"Suddenly a sound like the blowing of a violent wind came from heaven . . . They saw what seemed to be tongues of fire that separated and came to rest on each of them" (Acts 2:2, 3).

ENCOUNTER

The French philosopher and mathematician Blaise Pascal spoke of a "God-sized vacuum" in the heart of each man that can only be satisfied by God the Creator, made known through Jesus Christ. Only God's Spirit can fill the void in our souls.

The prophet Joel predicted the outpouring of the Holy Spirit eight hundred years before Christ. In Ezekiel 36:26, 27, God said, "I will give you a new heart and put a new spirit in you; I will remove from you your heart of stone and give you a heart of flesh. And I will put my Spirit in you." Jesus promised that His Spirit would come and will live inside those who believe in Him. ". . . The Comforter, which is the Holy Ghost, whom the Father will send in my name" (John 14:26, KJV). Jesus told the disciples, ". . . In a few days you will be baptized with the Holy Spirit" (Acts 1:5).

The early believers first experienced the outpouring. They heard a sound of heavenly fire like a violent hurricane but without the motion of wind. The day that God's Spirit came to them is celebrated as *Pentecost*, for the Greek word for fifty, as the day came fifty days after Jesus' Resurrection. God's Spirit poured out from high, like a lava flow that couldn't be contained, filling them with the Holy Spirit. "The wind blows wherever it pleases. You hear its sound, but you cannot tell where it comes from or where it is going. So it is with everyone born of the Spirit" (John 3:8).

The Comforter came and is here, to heal our anguish, to fill our empty hearts. That same filling occurs today, more or less dramatically. You may experience it as a tempest or as a calm. The outpouring of God's Spirit isn't a historic event, an ancient holiday, or religious rite. It occurs today. An individual experiences the spiritual birth when first he puts his trust in Christ.

The event is a real experience, a spiritual transformation, and a spiritual transfusion that occurs in a person's life the instant they receive Eternal Life. Rebirth is a life event that begins full communion and communication with God and distinguishes a Christian from a non-Christian. The difference is like that between a rose and a jewel. Both are beautiful, both are God's creation, but the rose is alive. A Christian is made alive at the second birth. "For as in Adam all die, so in Christ all will be made alive" (1 Corinthians 15:22). Having experienced rebirth, we can never be lost.

We look for God within—He's there only after experiencing the second birth. No one is born a Christian; you become one, when you're spiritually reborn. A miracle occurs in the soul, instantly, to whoever says yes to Christ. Then you live in God's presence and He lives in you. The term <u>enlightenment</u> falls short, implying merely knowledge or epiphany. God pours out His Spirit in almost a physical way. His essence is spiritual but real nonetheless.

PRAY: *"Comfort me, I need help. My heart is an empty vacuum. Transform me from a crystal rose to a living rose. Fill my heart with Your Spirit."*

DAY 27 — SUNDOWN The Spiritual Birth.

READING

". . . No one can see the kingdom of God unless he is born again" (John 3:3).

ENCOUNTER

Scripture speaks of six human states. The person who has been spiritually reborn will take **PATH A** to Eternal Life. One who dies without having been reborn will take **PATH B**.

PATH A	Pre-life	1st Birth (Physical)	2nd Birth (Spiritual Birth)	1st Death (Physical)	XXX	Resurrection (Eternal Life)
	(1.)	(2.)	(3.)	(4.)	(5.)	(6.)
PATH B	Pre-life	1st Birth (Physical)	XXX	1st Death (Physical)	2nd Death (Eternal Death)	XXX

(1.) Pre-life, preexistent state. From God's presence, our soul travels to earth in the ship of the body, the soul and mind put inside the flesh of an infant. (2.) The amniotic sac breaks; we slide through our dear mother's body to the place of muffled sounds— into the light of the 1st Birth.

(3.) 2nd Birth. The Second Birth may or not occur in your life. Nicodemus asked Jesus, in John 3:4, "Surely he cannot enter a second time into his mother's womb to be born?" Jesus said, ". . . No one can enter the kingdom of God unless he is born of water and the Spirit" (John 3:5). ". . . He saved us through the washing of rebirth and renewal by the Holy Spirit" (2 Titus 3:5). The second birth isn't with water. You become "born again," "born from above," "born of God," in spiritual rebirth. "I will give you a new heart and put a new spirit in you; I will remove from you your heart of stone and give you a heart of flesh. And I will put my Spirit in you" (Ezekiel 36:26, 27). I'm reborn when I trust in Christ. I get more than knowledge— God's Spirit lives in my body eternally. I'm aware of God in my life and of Jesus in His ascended state. I can fully walk in God's presence.

(4.) 1st Death. "And the dust returns to the ground it came from, and the spirit returns to God . . ." (Ecclesiastes 12:7). The soul is released back to the Creator when the body dies. "Have the gates of death been shown to you? Have you seen the gates of the shadow of death?" (Job 38:17). Near death, some die but return. There are many similar near-death or out-of-body experiences documented, where men see a light and then seem to cross a tunnel or bridge.

(5.) 2nd Death. Spiritual death of the soul. "And the devil, who deceived them, was thrown into the lake of burning sulfur, where the beast and the false prophet had been thrown. They will be tormented day and night for ever . . ." (Revelation 20:10). "Then death and Hades were thrown into the lake of fire . . . the second death" (Revelation 20:14). At the Second Death— for those who don't receive the Second Birth—the soul is banished from God and imprisoned. ". . . You do not believe that I am the one I claim to be, you will indeed die in your sins'" (John 8:24).

(6.) Resurrection (Eternal Life). The blissful hope for all who have received the Second or Spiritual Birth. "Blessed and holy are those who have part in the first resurrection. The second death has no power over them, but they will be priests of God and of Christ . . ." (Revelation 20:6).

PRAY: *"Through all means, through any means, save me from the Second Death."*

DAY 28 — DAYBREAK The Spiritual Transformation.

READING

". . . If anyone is thirsty, let him come to me and drink. Whoever believes in me, as the Scripture has said, streams of living water will flow from within him" (John 7:37, 38).

ENCOUNTER

Picture the volume of water pouring over Niagara or the half-mile cascade of Angel Falls. When God baptizes at the Second Birth, I'm sealed once and forever, like a deep cistern that overflows with endless streams of spiritual water pouring from my heart. God's Spirit lives in the new child of heaven, flowing like a thundering waterfall; as peaceful as a wave slipping back to sea breaking from shore. Jesus told a woman at Jacob's well that the Holy Spirit is like an endless supply of water. "If you knew the gift of God and who it is that asks you for a drink . . . The water I give him will become in him a spring of water welling up to eternal life" (John 4:10, 14).

Jesus' spiritual water comes from a deep well. A Christian has the power of the risen Christ and is transformed into a new person. How else to explain the success of The Walter Hoving Home in Garrison, New York? The Christ-based program claims an excellent recovery rate treating addicted women who have been transformed into new and inspiring individuals.

To be like Christ we let His nature, His Spirit, inside us take control. ". . . God has poured out his love into our hearts by the Holy Spirit, whom he has given us" (Romans 5:5). The Holy Spirit is a teacher, a guide, a comforter, enabling love, and other godly traits. Jesus said, "Remain in me, and I will remain in you. No branch can bear fruit by itself; it must remain in the vine. Neither can you bear fruit unless you remain in me. I am the vine; you are the branches. If a man remains in me and I in him, he will bear much fruit; apart from me you can do nothing" (John 15:4, 5).

The fruit of the Spirit manifests almost subconsciously by Christ's Spirit in a Christian. Fruit isn't produced by trying; fruit grows effortlessly by yielding to God's Spirit in us. The fruit doesn't grow from the branch but from the sap in the vine. Jesus is the vine and the Holy Spirit is the sap working inside a Christian. God puts His burning, aching heart for others in us. A heart of "flesh" replaces a heart of "stone." "I will give them an undivided heart and put a new spirit in them; I will remove from them their heart of stone and give them a heart of flesh" (Ezekiel 11:19).

God places the Holy Spirit's fruits supernaturally in the heart of a person who experiences the Second Birth. All the other fruits are rooted in love: "*Love— greatest of all, Joy cascades from Love's waterfall. Peace of God's power resting, Long-suffering Love's patience persevering. Gentleness is self-interest ignored, Goodness when Love's virtue adores. Faith is trust's convention, Meekness is Love in submission. Self-control, hesitation so perfect, Kindness Love compassionately sympathetic.*"

C. S. Lewis explained how improvement and transformation differ. "Improvement is not redemption, though redemption always improves people even here and now and will, in the end, improve them to a degree we cannot yet imagine. God became man to turn creatures into sons: not simply to produce better men of the old kind but to produce a new kind of man. It is not like teaching a horse to jump better and better but like turning a horse into a winged creature . . ." [14]

PRAY: *"Jesus, please transform me spiritually."*

DAY 28 — SUNDOWN The Spiritual Transformation.

READING

"Everyone who believes that Jesus is the Christ is born of God . . ." (1 John 5:1).

ENCOUNTER

In 1980 God arranged conditions for me to meet a Christian. After a deep talk, I was gripped by the issue, "Does God still speak to men?" I didn't know I could have a personal relationship with God. I sure didn't have one. God to me was a distant abstraction. He didn't exist, and I was miserable. I didn't experience the verse ". . . You will fill me with joy in your presence" (Psalm 16:11).

Unlikely coincidences began to occur that showed me God is real and that He was calling me. I found a meadow of poppies the same day I read a Bible verse about "lilies of the field" (Matthew 6:28). I was in a library researching diamonds and had an impulse to find a book about Jesus. I was shaken when I found these words in the first book about Jesus I opened.

"The study of the Bible is not unlike the search for diamonds in South Africa. At first people found a few diamonds in the yellow clay, and they were delighted with their good fortune, even while they supposed that this was to be the full extent of their find. Then, upon digging deeper, they came upon the blue clay, and, to their amazement, they then found as many precious stones in a day as they previously found in a year, and what formerly seemed like wealth faded into insignificance . . . In your exploration of Bible Truth, see that you don't rest satisfied in the yellow clay of a few spiritual discoveries, but press on to the rich blue clay underneath. The Bible, however, differs from the diamond field in the sublime fact that beneath the blue clay there are more and still more and richer strata . . . on and on to Infinity." [15]

These and other "chance" events were momentous and moved me to begin to believe in a living God. But I wasn't a Christian yet. I was intrigued by this verse, ". . . I am the way and the truth and the life. No one comes to the Father except through me" (John 14:6). One night I prayed to God, "If Jesus is Your Son, show me." In the early morning, I woke to a supernatural sound. I was so frightened my heart began pounding uncontrollably, as if I were having a heart attack. I felt and heard death near and I believe I would have died if I hadn't cried out, "Jesus, save me!"

In answer to my appeal to Jesus, God's Spirit poured out on me, and a voice spoke from within me, saying, "You are saved!" The words remind me of the truth of Romans 8:16: "The Spirit himself testifies with our spirit that we are God's children." I believe this Scripture describes what happened to me. " . . . He saved us, by the washing of regeneration, and renewing of the Holy Ghost; Which he shed on us abundantly through Jesus Christ our Saviour" (Titus 3:5, 6, KJV).

Afterward I felt a comforting "fullness" in my heart and abdomen, like a physical sensation, that wasn't there before. I found I had a newfound ability to cope with stress. Love for others replaced hate, by Christ's ability to love others through my heart. A week later, my urge to smoke vanished and I haven't smoked since. My phobia about death and dying began to lessen. I testify to you that something definitely changed in me. I was transformed. I know the Holy Spirit poured out on me that night. Since then, I'm slowly being transformed, a new creation, a spiritual son formed in the coursing waves of Spirit fire, until the day I meet Him, finally into the likeness of God.

PRAY: *"Jesus, save me!"*

DAY 29 — DAYBREAK His Deity.

READING

"God was manifest in the flesh" (1 Timothy 3:16, KJV).

"Simon Peter answered, 'You are the Christ, the Son of the living God'" (Matthew 16:16).

". . . We wait for the blessed hope— the glorious appearing of our great God and Savior, Jesus Christ" (Titus 2:13).

"The Son is the radiance of God's glory and the exact representation of his being, sustaining all things by his powerful word. After he had provided purification for sins, he sat down at the right hand of the Majesty in heaven" (Hebrews 1:3).

ENCOUNTER

There's a subplot in Sir Walter Scott's Ivanhoe where King Richard I (the Lion-Hearted) travels through England in disguise. He's evading his brother, the evil Prince John, who's in league with Richard's captor, the Duke of Austria. The effect when King Richard's identity is finally revealed is thrilling.

God, too, took on a cover. As a man, He exposed Himself to the pathetic conditions on earth. The Father sent Jesus to move among His creation, to interact person-to-person. Ask yourself, "If Jesus were only a prophet or religious leader, why does just saying His name invoke anger, fear, and resentment?" Because He said He was the only forgiver of sins, the only way to a relationship with God, and exclusion is offensive. He said, "He who hates me hates my Father as well" (John 15:23). If Jesus lied, how were demons cast out in His name then and today?

Once with His disciples Jesus took on a heavenly form. He ". . . took with him Peter, James and John the brother of James . . . up a high mountain by themselves. . . He was transfigured before them. His face shone like the sun, and his clothes became as white as the light" (Matthew 17:1, 2). God, from heaven, moved. ". . . A bright cloud enveloped them, and a voice from the cloud said, 'This is my Son, whom I love . . . Listen to him!'" (Matthew 17:5).

Daniel saw God's glory, purity, and power. "Thrones were set in place, and the Ancient of Days took his seat. His clothing was as white as snow; the **hair of his head was white like wool**. His throne was **flaming with fire** . . . A river of fire was flowing, coming out from before him. Thousands upon thousands attended him; ten thousand times ten thousand stood before him . . ." (Dan 7:9, 10, boldface mine).

Compare this picture of the ascended Jesus to the previous paragraph. "**His head and hair were white like wool**, as white as snow, and his eyes were like **blazing fire**. His feet were like bronze **glowing in a furnace**, and his voice was like the sound of rushing waters . . . His face was like the sun shining in all its brilliance . . . Then he placed his right hand on me and said: 'Do not be afraid. I am the First and the Last. I am the Living One; I was dead, and behold I am alive for ever and ever! And I hold the keys of death and Hades'" (Revelation 1:13-18, boldface mine). The Father in Daniel and the Son in Revelation are the same person.

PRAY: *"Jesus, my Lord and my God!"*

DAY 29 — SUNDOWN His Deity.

READING

"For in Christ all the fullness of the Deity lives in bodily form, and you have been given fullness in Christ, who is the head over every power and authority" (Colossians 2:9, 10).

"Who has gone up to heaven and come down? Who has gathered up the wind in the hollow of his hands? Who has wrapped up the waters in his cloak? Who has established all the ends of the earth? What is his name, and the name of his son? Tell me if you know!" (Proverbs 30:4).

ENCOUNTER

The above citations shout that God has a Son, that Jesus, the Son, is perfectly God. The morning of His crucifixion Jesus went before the Sanhedrin, the ruling body of Israel. ". . . the high priest asked him, 'Are you the Christ, the Son of the Blessed One?' 'I am,' said Jesus. 'And you will see the Son of Man sitting at the right hand of the Mighty One and coming on the clouds of heaven'" (Mark 14:61, 62). He could have lied to save Himself and the rulers would have released Him.

John 5:18 says they sought to kill him because he, ". . . was even calling God his own Father, making himself equal with God." Not only did He claim to be God's Son, He was tried and convicted of it. He said, in John 10:30, "I and the Father are one." "'We are not stoning you for any of these [miracles],' replied the Jews, 'but for blasphemy, because you, a mere man, claim to be God'" (John 10:33).

Saul, of the Sanhedrin, traveling to Damascus to apprehend Messianic Jews for trial, saw Jesus' glory in heaven, a glory that blinded him. ". . . Suddenly a light from heaven flashed around him. He fell to the ground and heard a voice say to him, 'Saul, Saul, why do you persecute me?' 'Who are you, Lord?' Saul asked. 'I am Jesus, whom you are persecuting . . ." (Acts 9:3-5).

The ascended Christ radically changed Saul [Paul], who was shipwrecked, beaten often, and finally killed for his new faith in Jesus. Only God can convert men. Paul's transformation proves the power of Christianity and Jesus' deity. Jesus can speak to you too, today— now— from heaven! He has risen. He's alive. Christians today receive divine revelation from Jesus Christ and are living proof that God changes lives. Each, like Saul, is an eyewitness whose testimony would hold up in court. Jesus is Lord. Call out to Him now and be changed!

Other spiritual leaders and political rulers were and are followed as gods, yet they're under condemnation as all other men. Only Jesus is the Son of God. "Salvation is found in no one else, for there is no other name under heaven given to men by which we must be saved" (Acts 4:12).

Paul said that Jesus possesses God's essence. "Who, being in the form of God, thought it not robbery to be equal with God" (Philippians 2:6, KJV). Thomas said, "My Lord and my God," the first time he saw Jesus alive after the resurrection, as written in John 20:28. Thomas worshipped Jesus when He apparently walked through walls into the room where the disciples were assembled. James finally believed in Him too, when he said about his half-brother, "Lord Jesus Christ, the Lord of Glory" (James 2:1, KJV).

PRAY: *"God, Scripture says that You have a Son. Jesus claims to be Your Son and many eyewitnesses proclaimed that He is. Perhaps the truth is that You, Jesus, <u>are</u> Lord."*

DAY 30 — DAYBREAK Perfect Justice and Mercy.

READING

". . . What shall we say? That God is unjust in bringing his wrath on us? . . . Certainly not! If that were so, how could God judge the world?" (Romans 3:5, 6).

ENCOUNTER

God is criticized for allowing disasters in the world and trouble in our lives. Some believe God is sadistic, cruel, and unfeeling. Others believe He's only a God of love, thinking, "God is too good to punish me." The Bible says that God wants the best for His creation and patiently waits for all to join Him in the afterlife, if it were possible. However, His own law binds Him to be perfectly just, righteous, and merciful. Sin comes at a price. Sin must be judged. God takes our sin, if we let Him, and places it on His own culpable Son, our substitute, to satisfy the law's judgment.

"Jesus took the Twelve aside and told them, 'We are going up to Jerusalem, and everything that is written by the prophets about the Son of Man will be fulfilled'" (Luke 18:31).

God's Righteousness. God is a righteous judge, obligated to punish each sin; to uphold consistently His own law. He cannot allow sin in His presence. "Do not think that I have come to abolish the Law or the Prophets; I have not come to abolish them but to fulfill them . . . until Heaven and earth disappear, not the smallest letter, not the least stroke of a pen, will by any means disappear from the Law until everything is accomplished" (Matthew 5:17, 18). There's no free pass. Someone has to pay for breaking the law. Either I pay or I can let Christ pay for me.

God's Judgment. The penalty for breaking God's law is punishment that fits the crime. God, as a concerned Father, corrects us by the events of life. "Because the Lord disciplines those he loves, and he punishes everyone he accepts as a son" (Hebrews 12:6).

Without stop signs, you don't need to stop at intersections. Without speed limits, you don't even know if you're going too fast. ". . . No one will be declared righteous in his sight by observing the law; rather, through the law we become conscious of sin" (Romans 3:20).

". . . Law brings wrath . . . where there is no law there is no transgression" (Romans 4:15).

". . . Call on a Father who judges each man's work impartially . . ." (1 Peter 1:17).

"For every living soul belongs to me, the father as well as the son— both alike belong to me. The soul who sins is the one who will die" (Ezekiel 18:4).

God's Vengeance. There's good reason not to strike back, yet it's difficult to be restrained. Let God avenge you. He says, ". . . 'It is mine to avenge; I will repay,' and again, 'The Lord will judge his people.' It is a dreadful thing to fall into the hands of the living God" (Hebrews 10:30).

"Whoever believes in the Son has eternal life, but whoever rejects the Son will not see life, for God's wrath remains on him" (John 3:36). Turn to Jesus, and turn away God's vengeance from you.

PRAY: *"My sense of justice is satisfied to know that every sin is punished."*

DAY 30 — SUNDOWN Perfect Justice and Mercy.

READING

". . . Man is destined to die once, and after that to face judgment" (Hebrews 9:27).

". . . Reserve the unjust unto the day of judgment to be punished" (2 Peter 2:9, KJV).

ENCOUNTER

If, as the Bible says, man dies only once, then reincarnation, being born into many lifetimes on Earth, doesn't happen. The Book of Revelation describes a record of our lives that God keeps for our judgment in the afterlife. "And I saw the dead, small and great, stand before God; and the books were opened; and another book was opened, which is the book of life. And the dead were judged out of those things which were written in the books, according to their works. And the sea gave up the dead which were in it, and death and hell delivered up the dead which were in them; and they were judged every man according to their works" (Revelation 20:12, 13, KJV).

You might feel that you're too good to be judged. After all, you've done nothing really wrong. Yet, as descendants of the human race, we live outside God's Eden. The demands of God's law won't allow sin to go unpunished. ". . . He has set a day when he will judge the world with justice by the man [Jesus] he has appointed. He has given proof of this to all men by raising him from the dead" (Acts 17:31).

Someday our motives, thoughts, and actions will be bared before God's scrutiny. Here's a picture of those who will be alive at the end of days: ". . . Every free man hid in caves and among the rocks of the mountains. They called to the mountains and the rocks, 'Fall on us and hide us from the face of him who sits on the throne and from the wrath of the Lamb! For the great day of their wrath has come, and who can stand?'" (Revelation 6:15-17).

If a person lives to eighty years, he's conscious one and a half billion seconds (excluding five years of childhood, and, say, eight hours of nightly sleep). All those opportunities for good or evil thoughts and actions will be brought before God's wisdom. Consider your responsibility for your deeds, as God will judge you (and even your thoughts) under His microscopic eye. "I am he who searches hearts and minds" (Revelation 2:23).

<u>God's Mercy</u>. God, like a parent, pursues us until we "find" Him. He wants that none will perish. "The Lord is not slow in keeping his promise . . . He is patient with you, not wanting anyone to perish, but everyone to come to repentance" (2 Peter 3:9). He offers a way out. We don't have to suffer wrath but can come under God's mercy and protection. ". . . I will have mercy on whom I have mercy, and I will have compassion on whom I have compassion" (Romans 9:15).

" . . . God, who is rich in mercy, made us alive with Christ even when we were dead in transgressions— it is by grace you have been saved" (Ephesians 2:4, 5).

"Let us then approach the throne of grace with confidence, so that we may receive mercy and find grace to help us in our time of need" (Hebrews 4:16).

PRAY: *"Thank You, Jesus, for taking the punishment for my sins. I kneel before Your throne. Thank You for Your mercy. Protect me from the full punishment of God's law."*

DAY 31 — DAYBREAK The Sacrifice.

READING

"Who gave himself for us to redeem us from all wickedness and to purify for himself a people that are his very own . . ." (Titus 2:14).

". . . The blood of Christ, who . . . offered himself unblemished to God, cleanse our consciences from acts that lead to death . . . Christ is the mediator of a new covenant" (Hebrews 9:14, 15).

ENCOUNTER

The Old Covenant says that God requires animal sacrifice by priests to cleanse sin. It's thought about twenty percent of the Torah (first five books of the Bible) speaks of sacrifices or *korbanot*. That concept seems archaic today, but in Jesus' time, temple sacrifices were still performed. The ancient offerings used various animals for different occasions. "This is what you are to offer on the altar regularly each day: two lambs a year old. Offer one in the morning and the other at twilight" (Exodus 29:38). Why sacrifice? ". . . To make an atonement for your souls" (Exodus 30:16, KJV).

On Yom Kippur, the Day of Atonement, two goats were taken. The scapegoat that bore the sins of the people was presented to God and then set free into the desert. "The goat will carry on itself all their sins to a solitary place . . ." (Leviticus 16:22). The other goat, the sin offering, was slain and used ritually. ". . . On that day shall the priest make an atonement for you, to cleanse you, that ye may be clean from all your sins before the Lord" (Leviticus 16:30, KJV).

Animal ritual predates the "once-for-all" sacrifice that Jesus made. Old Covenant sacrifice found fulfillment in Jesus Christ. God revealed to the prophet Jeremiah that He would issue a New Testament, ". . . I will make a new covenant with the house of Israel and with the house of Judah . . . For I will forgive their wickedness and will remember their sins no more" (Jeremiah 31:31, 34). Jesus and the New Testament ended animal sacrifice.

In the Old Covenant we read how Abraham and Sarah were promised a child. Because Sarah was well beyond her childbearing years, Isaac's birth was a miracle and a comfort to the elderly couple. Yet, while Abraham loved Isaac, he loved God more. That devotion to God would be tested when God gave Abraham the difficult command "to slay the boy." "Sacrifice him there as a burnt offering on one of the mountains I will tell you about" (Genesis 22:2). As they approached the offering place, Abraham with knife in hand, his son asked innocently, in Genesis 22:7, ". . . But where is the lamb for the burnt offering?"

Abraham didn't know how to answer. How could he murder his trusting child? "God himself will provide the lamb for the burnt offering, my son," he replied, in Genesis 22:8. When Abraham raised the knife over Isaac, he saw a ram, the substitute that God provided, caught in a thicket. Abraham would have slain Isaac for he knew "God could raise the dead" (Hebrews 11:19). Abraham offered the ram instead of his son and passed God's test of obedience.

Isaac set free symbolizes humanity forgiven. The ram is Christ, an infinitely holy substitute, a stand-in sacrifice for all people of all time. As Paul elaborated in Acts 17:2, 3, ". . . The Christ had to suffer and rise from the dead. 'This Jesus I am proclaiming to you is the Christ.'"

PRAY: *"Jesus, You are my substitute, God's eternal sacrifice."*

DAY 31 — SUNDOWN The Sacrifice.

READING

"Christ died for sins once for all, the righteous for the unrighteous, to bring you to God" (1 Peter 3:18).

"Such a high priest [Jesus] meets our need— one who is holy, blameless, pure, set apart from sinners, exalted above the heavens. Unlike the other high priests, he does not need to offer sacrifices day after day, first for his own sins, and then for the sins of the people. He sacrificed for their sins once for all when he offered himself" (Hebrews 7:26, 27).

"So Christ was sacrificed once to take away the sins of many people" (Hebrews 9:28).

". . . Made holy through the sacrifice of the body of Jesus Christ once for all" (Hebrews 10:10).

"But when this priest [Jesus] had offered for all time one sacrifice for sins, he sat down at the right hand of God" (Hebrews 10:12).

". . . By one sacrifice he has made perfect forever those . . . being made holy" (Hebrews 10:14).

ENCOUNTER

The Book of Hebrews explains Jesus' death as the just for the unjust. He ever fulfills the offerings required by Old Covenant law and the role of intercessor or intermediary to God as His sacrifice goes on and on. "Because Jesus lives forever, he has a permanent priesthood. Therefore he is able to save completely those who come to God through him, because he always lives to intercede for them" (Hebrews 7:24, 25).

Put a blemish on my face for every sin in my life and my features would deform beyond recognition. Then put my defects and those of everyone that ever lived on Jesus, the substitute, and sacrifice Him to end forever the daily rites of sacrifice. Mankind becomes cosmetically perfect, though the sin bearer is scarred by every vile offense of humanity.

"But he was pierced for our transgressions, he was crushed for our iniquities; the punishment that brought us peace was upon him, and by his wounds we are healed. We all, like sheep, have gone astray, each of us has turned to his own way; and the LORD has laid on him the iniquity of us all" (Isaiah 53:5, 6). Isaiah says this person will suffer for our sins to save us. As Rabbi Elijah de Vidas interprets Isaiah 53, ". . . since the Messiah bears our iniquities which produce the effect of His being bruised, it follows that whosoever will not admit that Messiah thus suffers for our iniquities, must endure and suffer them for himself." The Hebrew writer Yepheth ben Ali says of Isaiah 53, "That by the Messiah bearing them they would be delivered from the wrath which rested upon them." [16]

Our souls can be made clean by one sinless Person. Jesus died to end the need for animal sacrifice. Accept His sacrifice to receive pardon for sins, for always. ". . . We were God's enemies, we were reconciled to him through the death of his Son, how much more . . . saved through his life! . . . through whom we have now received reconciliation" (Romans 5:10, 11).

PRAY: *"Sinless One, You died for me!"*

DAY 32 — DAYBREAK The Blood.

READING

". . . The blood of Jesus, his Son, purifies us from all sin" (1 John 1:7).

ENCOUNTER

The first Passover shows the value of blood from God's view. As warned, the angel of death would strike down every first-born son, from those in Pharaoh's palace to those in the households of the Hebrew slaves.

To survive, God's people followed explicit instructions. On the tenth day of the month, each household took a perfect lamb. They slaughtered the lamb at twilight and drained the blood into a basin. They dipped hyssop into the basin and smeared the sides and tops of the doorframes of their houses.

". . . I will pass through Egypt and strike down every firstborn— both men and animals— and I will bring judgment on all the gods of Egypt. I am the LORD. The blood will be a sign for you on the houses where you are; and when I see the blood, I will pass over you. No destructive plague will touch you . . ." (Exodus 12:12, 13).

As Exodus 12:23 states, God's people were to be spared, for ". . . He will see the blood on the top and sides of the doorframe and will pass over that doorway, and he will not permit the destroyer to enter your houses and strike you down."

The blood was a sign to God which households had faith in Him. The believers marked the blood on the head of the doorway and spattered it on the two side jambs.

About midnight cries were heard throughout Egypt. Death avoided the sealed homes as the plague passed by them. But in Pharaoh's palace everyone and everything not covered by the blood died, including prisoners in their dungeons and livestock. That night demonstrated the power of blood to turn back God's just wrath. After leaving Egypt, Moses presented the law requiring continual animal slaughter to cover even the people's unintentional sins.

After Christ, however, animal offerings became pointless. Further sacrifice is unnecessary for believers in Jesus. His crucifixion paid the ultimate penalty for everyone. He substituted Himself, and He offers free and total forgiveness. ". . . God was reconciling the world to himself in Christ, not counting men's sins against them" (2 Corinthians 5:19).

When John the Baptist first saw Jesus he said, "Look, the Lamb of God, who takes away the sin of the world!" (John 1:29). Who was John? A prophet like Elijah who was sent to announce the coming of the Messiah, "See, I will send my prophet, who will prepare the way before me" (Malachi 3:1). Jesus validated John as that herald, in Luke 7:27, "This is the one about whom it is written 'I will send my messenger ahead of you, who will prepare your way before you.'" A prophet like Elijah will also herald the second coming of Messiah. "See, I will send you the prophet Elijah before that great and dreadful day of the LORD comes" (Malachi 4:5).

PRAY: *"Help me to understand that the blood of the first Passover lamb hinted of Christ's Easter sacrifice. That, Jesus' blood covers my sins and spares me from punishment."*

DAY 32 — SUNDOWN The Blood.

READING

"For the life of a creature is in the blood, and I have given it to you to make atonement for yourselves on the altar; it is the blood that makes atonement for one's life" (Leviticus 17:11).

"Though your sins are like scarlet, they shall be as white as snow; though they are red as crimson, they shall be like wool" (Isaiah 1:18).

". . . Wash me, and I will be whiter than snow" (Psalm 51:7).

". . . With the precious blood of Christ, a lamb without blemish or defect" (1 Peter 1:19).

ENCOUNTER

There are over five quarts of blood in the body. The fluid, red from oxygen, circulates in the heart, arteries, and veins. Blood carries gasses and dissolved substances to feed the brain and body. If allowed to drain out, death occurs in minutes, for the essence of life is in the blood.

From ancient days, shedding animal blood in the Jerusalem temple made atonement for sin. Animal sacrifice was an act of faith but the solution was temporary. When, in A. D. 70, the Romans destroyed the temple, the sacrifices ended. Even so, Jesus' atonement in A.D. 31 substituted once and forever, ending the need for all daily temple sacrifices.

"How much more, then, will the blood of Christ, who through the eternal Spirit offered himself unblemished to God, cleanse our consciences from acts that lead to death, so that we may serve the living God! For this reason Christ is the mediator of a new covenant, that those who are called may receive the promised eternal inheritance" (Hebrews 9:14, 15).

Eternal Life is freely available to those who accept that Jesus' death erases sins. If Christ's shed blood were only physical, then His death was insignificant. The spiritual effect of Christ's sacrifice provides an unstoppable source of cleansing.

Christ, who was sinless, has blood with eternal properties. Believers in Him, or those who choose to be washed in the cleansing, find He bleaches the stains on a human soul to absolute purity. Only an infinite God can take on the sins of all men and remove them.

Holy communion, which symbolizes atonement, is a ceremony to recall Christ's work. Jesus said, ". . . Do this, whenever you drink it, in remembrance of me. For whenever you eat this bread and drink this cup, you proclaim the Lord's death until he comes" (1 Corinthians 11:25, 26). Repeating the rite of communion isn't a condition for salvation. It's an act of remembrance and worship that Christ put daily animal sacrifice away. "Compulsory" rites of frequent communion shouldn't cheapen His death. He died once for all sins, past, present, and future.

I recall visiting a church before I found Jesus. I marveled at the inner peace of the partakers in the communion ceremony. I wished I could participate. I wanted peace. Now I have that peace and closeness to God.

PRAY: *"Oh His blood, His blood shed for me!"*

DAY 33 — DAYBREAK Forgiveness.

READING

"We have redemption through his blood, the forgiveness of sins" (Ephesians 1:7).

"When you were dead in your sins and in the uncircumcision of your sinful nature, God made you alive with Christ. He forgave us all our sins, having canceled the written code, with its regulations, that was against us and that stood opposed to us; he took it away, nailing it to the cross" (Colossians 2:13, 14).

"If we claim to be without sin, we deceive ourselves and the truth is not in us . . . He is faithful and just and will forgive us our sins and purify us from all unrighteousness" (1 John 1:8, 9).

"He is the atoning sacrifice for our sins, and not only for ours but also for the sins of the whole world" (1 John 2:2).

"He appeared so that he might take away our sins" (1 John 3:5).

ENCOUNTER

Are you laden with such guilt and shame that you can't let go? Our memories can be a cruel oppressor. Maybe this sounds familiar. ". . . My pain is ever with me. I confess my iniquity; I am troubled by my sin" (Psalm 38:17, 18). God wants to forgive you, no matter what you've done!

He sent His Son to cleanse you. Confession in prayer, between you and God, can bring relief. "Godly sorrow brings repentance that leads to salvation and leaves no regret . . ." (2 Corinthians 7:10). Jesus' death for the world's sin shows His selfless forgiveness. He altered the relationship of God to people forever. The Father chastised Jesus for our sins, satisfying the law and enabling us to regain God's good will. Jesus' atonement causes God to become favorably inclined toward men. He's appeased by the punishment of Jesus and so He forgives.

He says, in Psalm 103:12, "As far as the east is from the west, so far has he removed our transgressions from us," and in Jeremiah 31:34, ". . . I will forgive their wickedness and will remember their sins no more." The weight of our past is cut loose like a severed anchor sinking to the sea floor. We're free from accusation and guilt. His death makes us "Holy in his sight, without blemish and free from accusation" (Colossians 1:22).

When I realize that God forgives completely, I can forgive myself and be free from guilt. Then I can forgive others, which releases the pain of revenge I hold inside me.

"Doesn't unconditional forgiveness give me free license to sin when I want?" Paul says a resounding no! "What shall we say, then? Shall we go on sinning so that grace may increase? By no means! We died to sin; how can we live in it any longer?" (Romans 6:1, 2). Again, Romans 6:14, 15 says, "Sin shall not be your master, because you are not under law, but under grace. What then? Shall we sin because we are not under law but under grace? By no means!"

PRAY: *"Lord, I want to be set free from my sins, as You promise. Forgive me and take away the guilt that paralyzes me."*

DAY 33 — SUNDOWN Forgiveness.

READING

"You are forgiving and good, O Lord, abounding in love to all who call to you" (Psalm 86:5).

". . . In Christ God forgave you" (Ephesians 4:32).

". . . The Son of Man has authority on earth to forgive sins" (Matthew 9:6).

". . . He said to the paralytic, 'Take heart, son; your sins are forgiven'" (Matthew 9:2).

"Then Jesus said to her, 'Your sins are forgiven'" (Luke 7:48).

ENCOUNTER

Jesus has the authority and the power to forgive sins, and to bring us into perfect relationship with God. No one has the power to forgive sin but God Himself. Christ erases all sins, those "big" or "small". Jesus never committed a crime. Pilate said of Him, "I find no basis for a charge against him" (John 18:38). Yet He brought out hostility by claiming to be able to forgive sin.

You may say, "But, I'm not good enough or important enough to be forgiven!" No one is worthy. God offers grace, undeserved preferential treatment, to us. All is of God. None is of me.

Jesus said, in Mark 2:17, ". . . It is not the healthy who need a doctor, but the sick." He said in Matthew 9:13, ". . . I desire mercy, not sacrifice. For I have not come to call the righteous, but sinners."

Are you rejected?	God wants you.
Are you sick?	God can heal you.
Are you a sinner?	God will forgive you.
Are you hated?	God loves you.
Are you lonesome?	God is your Friend.

"Praise the LORD, O my soul; all my inmost being, praise his holy name. Praise the LORD, O my soul, and forget not all his benefits— who forgives all your sins and heals all your diseases . . ." (Psalm 103:1-3). He wants to forgive. He wants to forget.

We get forgiveness by turning from sin and asking God to restore our relationship with Him. A parent melts by the remorse of a child who says, "I'm sorry." God yearns to say, "I forgive you." "If we confess our sins, he is faithful and just and will forgive us our sins and purify us from all unrighteousness" (1 John 1:9).

He'll forgive you no matter what you've done. Remember the mercy He showed to those who were crucifying Him, saying, "Father, forgive them, for they do not know what they are doing" (Luke 23:33, 34). Once we accept Christ's forgiveness, our sins are forgotten. ". . . Forgetting what is behind and straining toward what is ahead, I press on toward the goal to win the prize for which God has called me heavenward in Christ Jesus" (Philippians 3:13, 14).

PRAY: *"I thank You that You forgive me for all that I've done."*

DAY 34 — DAYBREAK The Gift of Grace.

READING

". . . By grace you have been saved, through faith . . . it is the gift of God" (Ephesians 2:8).

"But when the kindness and love of God our Savior appeared, he saved us, not because of righteous things we had done, but because of his mercy" (Titus 3:4, 5).

ENCOUNTER

Do you believe in luck or consider yourself lucky? Maybe you survived a critical illness or had a near-death experience. Perhaps you walked away from an accident that should have killed you. You may have experienced an unexplained act of probability or a miracle. The right answer you need always seems to come.

Your "luck" may be God's providence. His unseen hand guides us benevolently. His intervention in our lives is part of His grace, His divine favor. He even sends angels to watch over and protect us.

Sir Isaac Newton's Third Law of Motion states, "For each action there is an equal and opposite reaction." Similarly, the Buddhist law of Karma says each event is caused by a prior event. The spiritual world is as real as the physical world and has its own principles. There are reactions in the spiritual world, behind the scenes, to our every action. That gives power to prayer. We pray, and if our words touch God's heart, He may will to grant our request.

Some philosophies unknowingly uncover God's spiritual truths. God's absolutes work even if He doesn't get the credit. For example, positive thinking is a belief system that works because it's based on this biblical truth, "Do not be anxious about anything, but in everything, by prayer and petition, with thanksgiving, present your requests to God. And the peace of God, which transcends all understanding, will guard your hearts and your minds in Christ Jesus . . . whatever is true, whatever is noble, whatever is right, whatever is pure, whatever is lovely, whatever is admirable— if anything is excellent or praiseworthy— think about such things" (Philippians 4:6-8).

Grace is a gift, an offering of love. Grace is favor, unearned, unwarranted, unexpected, and unmerited. Grace is given freely. "For just as the Father raises the dead and gives them life, even so the Son gives life to whom he is pleased to give it" (John 5:21). "No one knows who the Son is except the Father, and no one knows who the Father is except the Son and those to whom the Son chooses to reveal him" (Luke 10:22). The key word is <u>chooses</u>. God chooses to love us.

The need of the recipient determines the gift's relevance and its value but not its cost. The need of humanity is most urgent and most dear. God responded to our poverty by offering His Son as a gift for everyone. The Good News is that Eternal Life doesn't need to be earned. Eternity is revealed to whoever will accept Jesus. Like any gift, you must receive Eternal Life to keep it. When you receive the gift, heaven reacts to your act of faith.

Jesus first died for us. ". . . While we were still sinners, Christ died for us" (Romans 5:8). Fortunately, He shows us the method, the path that leads to salvation.

PRAY: *"Thank You that Eternal Life is a gift. There's nothing I need do but accept the gift gladly."*

DAY 34 — SUNDOWN The Gift of Grace.

READING

"For the law was given through Moses; grace and truth came through Jesus Christ" (John 1:17).

"The gift of God is eternal life in Christ Jesus our Lord" (Romans 6:23).

ENCOUNTER

We all want to live after death. That desire has fueled the cryogenics movement, which offers the hope that a human corpse may be preserved by freezing in super-cooled liquid nitrogen until science learns how to restore life to it. Yet the body is a shell for our soul and only a temporary home. In Mary Shelley's Frankenstein, the narrator presents the hope to restore life after death, the hope of humanity.

"After days and nights of incredible labour and fatigue, I succeeded in discovering the cause of generation and life; nay, more, I became myself capable of bestowing animation upon lifeless matter . . . What had been the study and desire of the wisest men since the creation of the world was now within my grasp . . . I was like the Arabian who had been buried with the dead and found a passage to life, aided only by one glimmering and seemingly ineffectual light . . . If I could bestow animation upon lifeless matter, I might in process of time (although I now found it impossible) renew life where death had apparently devoted the body to corruption." [17]

Of course, Shelley's narrative is fiction. The real person inside the flesh moves on after death. Not worth preserving, bodily remains can be discarded. Eternal Life can't be manufactured for eternity is God's gift. Don't cling to the physical when only the spiritual has lasting value.

God offers today— now— the gift of Eternal Life by accepting for our own Jesus' sacrifice through His crucifixion. Only God can change men. Eternal Life is the result of having been rescued. Rebirth is a spiritual transformation. The gift is priceless. Grace cost the Son of God a brutal, substituted death.

Everlasting Life is a gift that can't be bought because it's God's gift to us. If you believe in the giver, then take the gift. Eternal Life must be accepted from the giver before the prize becomes your own.

The thief crucified next to Jesus couldn't buy Eternal Life. Even if it were possible to work our way to heaven, the thief had no time left to do enough good to make up for a lifetime of sins. The thief repented and believed. He pleaded, in Luke 23:42, "Jesus, remember me when you come into your kingdom."

"Jesus answered him, 'I tell you the truth, today you will be with me in paradise'" (Luke 23:43). By believing in Christ, even moments before he died, Christ gave him a full pardon. The reprieve was God's gift.

The law has no greater penalty than death. Jesus had to pay with His life because He was guilty of my sin. His death was His gift to me. He died in my place.

PRAY: *"I humbly accept Your gift. I honestly don't know what other choice I have."*

DAY 35 — DAYBREAK The Faith.

READING

". . . Faith comes from hearing . . . and the message is heard through the word of Christ" (Romans 10:17).

ENCOUNTER

"The apostles said to the Lord, 'Increase our faith!'" (Luke 17:5). Ask God for faith. He's happy to increase your faith for, as the writer says in Hebrews 11:6, ". . . Without faith it is impossible to please God, because anyone who comes to him must believe that he exists and that he rewards those who earnestly seek him." Faith and reason are complementary. "Love the Lord your God with all your heart and with all your soul and with all your mind and with all your strength" (Mark 12:30). Jesus says to use your intellect. Yet faith carries on where reason ends.

There's little physical proof, yet there's enough historical testimony written in biblical and nonbiblical sources of reliable eyewitnesses that would be sustained in court as evidence for God's existence. ". . . Just as they were handed down to us by those who from the first were eyewitnesses and servants of the word . . . since I myself have carefully investigated everything from the beginning, it seemed good also to me to write an orderly account for you" (Luke 1:2, 3).

We boost our faith by hearing and reading the Bible. A good starting place is the Book of John. Some radio and TV shows broadcast God's truth. But be wary of phonies who exalt themselves or emphasize donations— no matter how sincere or urgent their pleas.

Attend a Bible-believing church, one where Christ is worshipped as Savior and Lord. Find a place where you won't be asked to give your money, time, or services in return for grace or to get some spiritual advantage. There are false churches of all denominations, though Christians may be found in any denomination. I don't endorse a denomination. I declare Christ!

"I don't want to go to church. Church is filled with all those hypocrites!" The animated preacher Billy Sunday's answer was, "So's Hell. I say to you if you don't want to go to Hell and live with that bunch forever, come into the church where you won't have to associate with them very long. There are no hypocrites in Heaven." [18]

Religion isn't spirituality. Spirituality is a relationship. Christ links you to God. Christianity isn't a religion, but it is a divine revelation. God doesn't require religious acts or rites, though I'm convinced that God is thrilled to receive our devotions as an act of love. He's into relationships—from the heart— with people. And He is into faith. Yet if a person is spiritually transformed, he naturally will want, and need, to be with people who are also changed.

". . . Anyone who will not receive the kingdom of God like a little child will never enter it" (Luke 18:17). The reason is that, a child has natural trust. A toddler takes his first faltering steps to his parent. The faith of youth is simple. "Abram believed the LORD, and he [God] credited it to him as righteousness" (Genesis 15:6). "Through him you believe in God, who raised him from the dead and glorified him, and so your faith and hope are in God" (1 Peter 1:21).

PRAY: *"I need assurance that all this is true. Lord, strengthen my faith."*

DAY 35 — SUNDOWN The Faith.

READING

"Now faith is being sure of what we hope for and certain of what we do not see" (Hebrews 11:1).

"By faith we understand that the universe was formed at God's command, so that what is seen was not made out of what was visible" (Hebrews 11:3).

"Who through faith conquered kingdoms" (Hebrews 11:33).

ENCOUNTER

Having faith doesn't imply being brainless. Faith isn't blind; it's based on evidence and reason. But logic won't take you all the way. You must take a "leap of faith," a leap into the light, to be certain. And faith isn't earned, it's given to you! It's God's gift to you.

Moses was a man of faith and God spoke to him. "By faith Moses, when he had grown up, refused to be known as the son of Pharaoh's daughter. He chose to be mistreated along with the people of God rather than to enjoy the pleasures of sin for a short time. He regarded disgrace for the sake of Christ as of greater value than the treasures of Egypt, because he was looking ahead to his reward. By faith he left Egypt, not fearing the king's anger; he persevered because he saw him who is invisible" (Hebrews 11:24-27).

Is God invisible to you? Faith in Christ is more than a psychological action where you just deceive yourself into believing. Faith is real and faith is based on objective truth. There is miraculous evidence of God in the modern world: There are encounters with angels, healings, exorcisms, and spiritual rebirth. We see continued fulfillment of prophesy, like the reestablished State of Israel, and events even more stunning will take place in the Holy Land in the future. And the world will see Jesus' return.

Faith isn't a spiritual aptitude to be strived for or perfected. Faith isn't tangible. True faith isn't confidence in me or in my faith. That kind of faith is a pitfall. That's ME-based, rather than GOD-based. Faith should be aroused from a place of dependency, from weakness, not strength. Faith mustn't be from me, but it must be in God.

"This righteousness from God comes through faith in Jesus Christ to all who believe . . ." (Romans 3:22). Faith is released at whatever level I can consciously summon it forth. There's a faith that saves. "Your faith has saved you" (Luke 7:50).

". . . Faith is credited as righteousness" (Romans 4:5). "Justified through faith, we have peace with God through our Lord Jesus Christ, through whom we have gained access by faith . . ." (Romans 5:1, 2).

". . . Found in him, not having a righteousness of my own that comes from the law, but that which is through faith in Christ— the righteousness that comes from God and is by faith" (Philippians 3:9).

PRAY: *"I need You, even to increase my faith. I believe in You to provide my next breath, my next meal, my mate, my income, my release from pain, my today, my tomorrow, and my afterlife."*

DAY 36 — DAYBREAK Surrender.

READING

"Yet to all who received him, to those who believed in his name, he gave the right to become children of God" (John 1:12, emphasis mine).

ENCOUNTER

I'm not God! Neither am I a god. A human is a proud individual, but the day arrives when we must realize and admit there's a Supreme Being. God took care of my birth. He gave me identity. He didn't need to create me; I do things His way or I must pay for my rebellion. So I lay down my will to His. It's better to bend than break.

God's way is humbling. We must surrender our own righteousness, admit we're spiritually bankrupt, and accept Christ's righteousness. We must believe it in our mind, but facts are not enough. Next, we must receive it into our heart, for love is an act of the will. Imagine loving your mother with your mind but not with your heart! You become God's child through the heart.

Believe in Him

"That if you confess with your mouth, 'Jesus is Lord,' and believe in your heart that God raised him from the dead, you will be saved" (Rom 10:9).

"Everyone who believes that Jesus is the Christ is born of God . . ." (1 John 5:1).

". . . Everyone who looks to the Son and believes in him shall have eternal life, and I will raise him up at the last day" (John 6:40).

". . . He who believes has everlasting life" (John 6:47)

We surrender to Him. We cease our fruitless struggling. We must take the leap of faith into the light and believe.

Receive Him

We exercise our will and give over our life by acknowledging God's lordship and His Son's deity. When we take His way to our heart, our sins are forgiven. His Holy Spirit fills our heart.

". . . Everyone who believes in him receives forgiveness of sins through his name" (Acts 10:43).

Become God's Child

". . . Unless you change and become like little children, you will never enter the kingdom of heaven" (Matthew 18:3).

We become Christians by believing thoughtfully, and receiving emotionally, in childlike faith. Giving up our status as "number one," we must give in to become a child of God.

PRAY: *"I ask You with my heart to come into my life. Give me the faith to believe that I may be reborn from above."*

DAY 36 — SUNDOWN Surrender.

READING

"Don't you know me, Philip, even after I have been among you such a long time? Anyone who has seen me has seen the Father . . ." (John 14:9).

"You call me 'Teacher' and 'Lord,' and rightly so, for that is what I am" (John 13:13).

ENCOUNTER

In March 1977 an aviation disaster involved two Boeing 747s on the ground at Tenerife, in the Canary Islands. Seconds before the collision, the pilot lifting off couldn't believe what he saw emerging out of the fog. Blocking the runway was the fuselage of a taxiing jet! The flight recorder held the epitaph of the pilot who frantically and hopelessly strained his aircraft over the other that straddled the runway. In that urgent moment, the last sound on the voice recorder was a scream.

If I wait to reach out to God thinking I'll make my peace later, I'm kidding myself. Will you wait to make your decision about eternity on your deathbed? Our response is crucial. If your heart is soft now, then don't delay. Your heart may be hard tomorrow. And do you know that you will even have tomorrow?

How should I respond? Is my response one of reverence and surrender or do I retreat from God? God risks rejection by approaching us first, by showing us evidence in physical nature, in the Bible, and by having sent ahead an emissary, His Son.

We may be singled out for attention by God, known by Him, noticed. Only by His recognition of us do we become important for all time. Our lives are meaningful when we carry out God's plan. He calls out to us to acknowledge the supremacy of His will over ours. Will I respect His wisdom and authority?

He did all He possibly could do for us. Romans 5:10 says, "For if, when we were God's enemies, we were reconciled to him through the death of his Son, how much more, having been reconciled, shall we be saved through his life!"

What does He have to do to win our love? What wall must come down from around my heart that will let me trust and yield? Submit or turn away, possibly forever, with tears of regret.

You may ask, "Why should I follow a Jewish prophet and a Christian God?" True, Jesus' mother Mary (Miriam) was Jewish, but His Father was God. His unique birth makes Jesus the "universal" man for all nations. He's related to all people through God and to all people through Adam and Eve.

Receive Jesus in simplicity as Lord and as Savior. And, having done that, rejoice that you're reborn. ". . . Do not rejoice that the spirits submit to you, but rejoice that your names are written in heaven" (Luke 10:20).

PRAY: *"Teacher, Lord, Father, I believe. I surrender."*

DAY 37 — DAYBREAK Certitude and Peace.

READING

"I write these things to you who believe in the name of the Son of God so that you may know that you have eternal life" (1 John 5:13).

"For he has set a day when he will judge the world with justice by the man he has appointed. He has given proof of this to all men by raising him from the dead" (Acts 17:31).

ENCOUNTER

When the Holy Spirit comes upon us, on the first day of our salvation, the experience is real. He comes into our heart, allowing us to say, "*Abba*," "Father," "Daddy" (Galatians 4:6). After the event of our salvation, in our heart we feel assured that God is our Father.

The fulfillment of ancient prophecies supports the truth of God and the Bible. When the Bible is read with the light of the Holy Spirit for guidance and interpretation, its authority is compelling. Truth can be debated but not refuted, and the Bible is ultimate Truth.

Before we die, we must know we own Eternal Life or we may not have it! Once we believe that Jesus is the Christ and that God raised Him from the dead, then we know we are reborn. God assures us through intimacy with the resurrected Christ.

Our act of faith is rewarded with a new certainty, the peace of knowing truth. Faith becomes reality. Christians live on a special plane where heaven and earth intersect, with a spiritual discernment that God is real! Certitude frees me to live in the reality of heaven.

Can you lose your salvation? Let's be honest. If there were a way to lose salvation, man would find the way. God doesn't expect perfection from mortals. He sent His Son to cover for our faults and weaknesses.

"I give them eternal life, and they shall never perish; no one can snatch them out of my hand" (John 10:28). We can never again be lost once we're found.

". . . I am not ashamed, because I know whom I have believed, and am convinced that he is able to guard what I have entrusted to him for that day" (2 Timothy 1:12). Though I can't maintain my faith, or certitude, or peace, or holiness, He's able to keep me in a safe state perpetually!

". . . There is now no condemnation for those who are in Christ Jesus, because through Christ Jesus the law of the Spirit of life set me free from the law of sin and death" (Romans 8:1, 2).

PRAY: *"God, in a world of uncertainty and anxiety, I need certitude from You because life without assurance is insecure. I need peace even more than life."*

DAY 37 — SUNDOWN Certitude and Peace.

READING

"Peace I leave with you; my peace I give you. I do not give to you as the world gives. Do not let your hearts be troubled and do not be afraid" (John 14:27).

"I have told you these things, so that in me you may have peace. In this world, you will have trouble. But take heart! I have overcome the world" (John 16:33).

ENCOUNTER

Maybe you've been hurting on the inside. Jesus gives His disciples tangible inner peace and comfort, and the ability to cope with life. He promises the peace of God that exceeds understanding. "You will keep in perfect peace him whose mind is steadfast, because he trusts in you" (Isaiah 26:3). There are different types of peace:

Peace in the individual. In the core of our being, one needs to feel safe from outside forces. Peace must begin in hearts for the world to be at peace. The peace Christ gives is to the person first. There are extreme life situations that can be borne only if we know Christ.

You ask, "Do you think I'm so feeble that I need a crutch?" Asking God for peace isn't a sign of weakness. Dependency on God is normal life, life as God intended.

Peace in the family. In broken families, God, through Jesus Christ, can reestablish marriages. Discipline and respect can be restored in our homes. "Honor your father and your mother" is a key commandment from Exodus 20:12, as is "Fathers, do not exasperate your children," from Ephesians 6:4.

Peace in the nation. Pray for those in authority. Pray for the return of godliness and holiness in our own life, in our homeland, and among our leaders.

Peace among countries. This world so longs for peace. The optimism of the industrial, electronic, and information ages has faded. Technology should have brought freedom and perfection. Instead, there are soaring populations, food crises, pollution, loss of the ozone layer, religious and racial wars, terrorists that have cheapened life, those that will not hesitate to use any high-tech weapon they can. Stability has never been threatened more. High-tech weapons may destroy civilization.

Jesus warned about the end times. He said there will be a tidal wave of immorality. There will be strife that jeopardizes world peace. Those days will test God's elected ones when the antichrist rises to power. "Don't let anyone deceive you in any way, for that day will not come until the rebellion occurs and the man of lawlessness is revealed . . ." (2 Thessalonians 2:3).

". . . All authority in heaven and on earth has been given to me . . . And surely I am with you always, to the very end of the age" (Matthew 28:18, 20). Jesus says, "I have overcome the world." Our world. My world. Find peace in His words.

PRAY: *"Jesus I want the peace and the power You promise. A supernatural peace, not a self-willed, forced peace that's circumstantial and can't last. I want and need lasting peace."*

DAY 38 — DAYBREAK The Apocalypse.

READING

". . . 'Tell us,' they said, 'when will this happen, and what will be the sign of your coming and of the end of the age?'" (Matthew 24:3).

ENCOUNTER

Jesus' disciples wanted to know, as we do, when the end of time will come. Included in Matthew 24, Mark 13, and Luke 21 (paraphrased below) are Jesus' list of signs for us.

False Christs will arise.

Signs and wonders will appear.

Nations will incur aggression.

There will be wars and impending wars.

There will be widespread famine and pestilence.

We will see fearful sights in the heavens.

Earthquakes will occur.

"While people are saying, 'Peace and safety,' destruction will come on them suddenly, as labor pains on a pregnant woman, and they will not escape" (1 Thessalonians 5:3). The beginning of birth pains is slow and less intense. In the final moments before the end time approaches, the labor pain of the earth will become more frequent and unbearable.

Affliction will rise more than ever.

An increase of troubles, in intensity and frequency, will be seen.

Christians will be hated, persecuted, betrayed, jailed, and killed for their faith.

Brothers will betray brothers.

Children will betray their parents.

Many will turn away from God.

False prophets will deceive the masses.

Iniquity shall be rampant and men will be ungodly.

The love for God will wane.

There will be little or no belief in Christ's return.

The anitichrist, claiming to be God, will deceive the earth.

The Good News of Jesus Christ will be preached in the entire world (e.g., radio, TV, the Internet) and then the end shall come. Daniel predicted that at the end of time knowledge would increase. ". . . The time of the end. Many will go here and there to increase knowledge" (Daniel 12:4). We're in the age of information. The Internet makes the collective knowledge and wisdom of the world available to all.

The prophet Joel wrote of the last days of God, saying, "I will show wonders in the heavens and on the earth, blood and fire and billows of smoke. The sun will be turned to darkness and the moon to blood before the coming of the great and dreadful day of the LORD. And everyone who calls on the name of the LORD will be saved . . ." (Joel 2:30-32).

PRAY: *"God, save me from perishing in the time of the end."*

DAY 38 — SUNDOWN The Apocalypse.

READING

"But the day of the Lord will come like a thief. The heavens will disappear with a roar; the elements will be destroyed by fire, and the earth and everything in it will be laid bare" (2 Peter 3:10).

"I watched as he opened the sixth seal. There was a great earthquake. The sun turned black like sackcloth made of goat hair, the whole moon turned blood red, and the stars in the sky fell to earth, as late figs drop from a fig tree when shaken by a strong wind" (Revelation 6:12, 13).

"There will be signs in the sun, moon and stars. On the earth, nations will be in anguish and perplexity at the roaring and tossing of the sea. Men will faint from terror, apprehensive of what is coming on the world, for the heavenly bodies will be shaken" (Luke 21:25, 26).

". . . That day will close on you unexpectedly like a trap. For it will come upon all those who live on the face of the whole earth" (Luke 21:34, 35).

ENCOUNTER

The beast of Daniel 7:11 is also known as the antichrist. "Dear children, this is the last hour; and as you have heard that the antichrist is coming, even now many antichrists have come. This is how we know it is the last hour" (1 John 2:18).

The prophecy of the beast has yet to happen. He will be a "man of peace," a false charismatic messiah who will bring three and a half years of world peace. "The beast was given a mouth to utter proud words and blasphemies and to exercise his authority for forty-two months" (Revelation 13:5). The brief time of peace will be followed by three and a half years of the worst time in history, called the Great Tribulation in Revelation 7:14.

The beast will be overthrown, as will the devil. "But the beast was captured, and with him the false prophet who had performed the miraculous signs on his behalf . . . The two of them were thrown alive into the fiery lake of burning sulfur" (Revelation 19:20).

In the end time, just before Christ returns bodily, these events will mark the Apocalypse: (Please see the Appendix for more details.)

A major earthquake will occur.

The sun will blacken and the moon will appear as blood.

Typhoons will rage, the seas will roar, and a tidal wave will engulf the coasts.

The powers of the heavens will be shaken and the stars of heaven will fall to the earth.

The "day of the Lord" will arrive.

Heaven will pass away, like a scroll imploding inward.

The Son of God will return, appearing from the east on clouds.

Jesus will gather His people from the four corners of the earth.

The elements will melt down as intense heat engulfs and burns planet Earth.

"Then the end will come, when he [Jesus] hands over the kingdom to God the Father after he has destroyed all dominion, authority and power" (1 Corinthians 15:24).

PRAY: *"God, I thank You that I can escape the seven-year tribulation and judgment."*

DAY 39 — DAYBREAK Hell and Heaven.

READING

". . . Depart from me, you who are cursed, into the eternal fire prepared for the devil and his angels" (Matthew 25:41).

ENCOUNTER

There's an account in Luke 16 about a rich man and Lazarus, a beggar. Lazarus died and went to heaven. The rich man also died and through the flames of hell, he could see Lazarus, in comfort, across an impassable gulf. The rich man was helpless to change his situation but cried out, in Luke 16:27, 28, ". . . I beg you, father, send Lazarus to my father's house, for I have five brothers. Let him warn them, so that they will not also come to this place of torment."

We speculate about the conditions in hell, for hell is also Eternal Life, yet a place of eternal nightmare. The Psalmist alludes to "the sorrows of hell" (Psalm 18:5, KJV).

"If anyone's name was not found written in the book of life, he was thrown into the lake of fire" (Revelation 20:15). The Greek word used for fire is pyre. Hell is described as a place where the inhabitants are ". . . suffering the vengeance of eternal fire" (Jude 1:7, KJV). Imagine the glaring surface of the moon at midday, or Jupiter, stormy and arid. Thirst without relief. Heat without end. Steam scalding the skin and body. Burning horrors like a crashing, blazing aircraft. Wind storms that sear and bring no promise of relief. Hissing gasses that choke. ". . . The fiery furnace, where there will be weeping and gnashing of teeth" (Matthew 13:42).

Perhaps it's a place that's always pitch black. Once I visited an underground cavern. The guide turned off the only light to give the tourists a sense of total darkness. Fortunately, the lights went on in a few seconds just as we were getting anxious in the blackness. "Cast out into outer darkness; there shall be weeping and gnashing of teeth" (Matthew 8:12, KJV).

There will be alienation from God, His love, and His other attributes. ". . . Punished with everlasting destruction and shut out from the presence of the Lord and from the majesty of his power" (2 Thessalonians 1:9).

There will be spiritual emptiness, nonstop terror, and a sense of evil and foreboding. Lost human souls and horrendous creatures will cohabitate. Demons, perhaps with hideous voices screaming, gurgling, and cackling, will be present. Picture an endless nightmare Halloween with everlasting torture.

Madness and psychosis are sure to follow as the memories, the regret of mortal life repeat endlessly, forming deep ruts of melancholy. Uncontrollable thoughts will race toward distress, anxiety, fear, and panic. Anger fuels depression, remorse becomes hatred, and hatred fuels more anger.

The Bible calls hell "this place of torment" (Luke 16:28). "And the smoke of their torment rises for ever and ever. There is no rest day or night . . ." (Revelation 14:11).

PRAY: *"God, save me from a life worse than life on earth, hell."*

DAY 39 — SUNDOWN Hell and Heaven.

READING

"Do not let your hearts be troubled. Trust in God; trust also in me. In my Father's house are many rooms . . . I am going there to prepare a place for you" (John 14:1, 2).

ENCOUNTER

The Bible says heaven is better than anything we imagine. ". . . No eye has seen, no ear has heard, no mind has conceived what God has prepared for those who love him" (1 Corinthians 2:9). I've heard said that the first time we see heaven, our reaction will be, "Oh, of course!"

"Then I saw a new heaven and a new earth, for the first heaven and the first earth had passed away . . ." (Revelation 21:1).

God will dwell with His people. ". . . God himself shall be with them, and be their God" (Revelation 21:3, KJV). "He will wipe every tear from their eyes. In heaven, there will be no more death or mourning or crying or pain, for the old order of things has passed away" (Revelation 21:4). There will be no more anguish and no more tears.

"The twelve gates were twelve pearls, each gate made of a single pearl. The great street of the city was of pure gold, like transparent glass" (Revelation 21:21). Revelation 21:12 tells of a high wall with an angel at each of the twelve gates. "The foundations of the city walls were decorated with every kind of precious stone" (Revelation 21:19). This illustration shows the gems of heaven's foundation.

GEM	FOUNDATION		GEM	FOUNDATION
Sardius (Carnelian)	6th foundation		Amethyst	12th foundation
Sardonyx (Onyx)	5th foundation		Jacinth	11th foundation
Emerald	4th foundation		Chrysoprase	10th foundation
Chalcedony (Agate)	3rd foundation		Topaz	9th foundation
Sapphire	2nd foundation		Beryl	8th foundation
Jasper	1st foundation		Chrysolite	7th foundation

"And the one who sat there had the appearance of jasper and carnelian. A rainbow, resembling an emerald, encircled the throne" (Revelation 4:3).

There will be no night, so no need for sleep. "I did not see a temple in the city, because the Lord God Almighty and the Lamb are its temple. The city does not need the sun or the moon to shine on it, for the glory of God gives it light, and the Lamb is its lamp" (Revelation 21:22, 23). We'll inherit immortal bodies that won't hurt, become sick, or die and we'll be able to see God, as He is.

I long to stride down heaven's platinum avenues. To explore this universe and others. To know and love all its residents intimately. To worship God. To play guitar far better than was ever heard on earth. To sing in a beautiful voice without embarrassment. To have perfect relationships not marred by conflict or sin. And, I hope to reunite with the departed that I've loved.

PRAY: *"Lord, give me assurance that heaven is real and that You reserve a place for me there."*

DAY 40 — DAYBREAK The Love of God.

READING

"Very rarely will anyone die for a righteous man, though for a good man someone might possibly dare to die. But God demonstrates his own love for us in this: While we were still sinners, Christ died for us" (Romans 5:7, 8).

"Greater love has no one than this, that he lay down his life for his friends" (John 15:13).

ENCOUNTER

Young, solitary Sydney Carton went resolutely to the guillotine in Charles Dickens's A Tale of Two Cities. He replaced Charles Darnay, his look-alike friend, who had a family, a man whose death would be tragic. The innocent Carton and another speak as they await the blade.

"Are you dying for him?" she whispered. "And his wife and child?"

"Hush! Yes!"

"O you will let me hold your brave hand, stranger?"

"Hush! Yes, my poor sister, to the last." [19]

"But for you, dear stranger, I should not be so composed, for I am naturally a poor little thing, faint of heart; nor should I have been able to raise my thoughts to Him who was put to death, that we might have hope and comfort here to-day. I think you were sent to me by heaven." [20]

Carton's act of substitution for Darnay helps show God's true, unconditional, and sacrificial love. Jesus, too, died for people. The King gave His life for His subjects, those that He loved most. He bought others' happiness with His own death. He came to give and not receive. Jesus substituted for those He loves. He relieved the condemned.

We can respond to His sacrifice by freely giving back our lives to Him. Yet a person isn't innately sacrificial without the indwelling Holy Spirit. Without God's Spirit living in me, trying to be religious is toil, not joy. Pure religion is brittle, monastic, and strained.

Jesus experienced the savage crowd's delight at His death that Good Friday. But He was selfless. He ignored the pain, the melancholy, the thoughts of his draining strength and impending death. He even paid for the sins of the bloodthirsty crowd. He rescued those who didn't know they needed deliverance, for everyone needs to be redeemed.

The greatest attribute is love. If I "have not love, I am nothing" (1 Corinthians 13:2).

Love never fails. God never fails.

PRAY: *"Father, loose me from the prison of religion by freeing my soul into true and unbridled spirituality of love."*

DAY 40 — SUNDOWN The Love of God.

READING

". . . With all the saints, to grasp how wide and long and high and deep is the love of Christ, and to know this love that surpasses knowledge . . ." (Ephesians 3:18, 19).

"God is love" (1 John 4:8).

"This is love: not that we loved God, but that he loved us and sent his Son as an atoning sacrifice for our sins" (1 John 4:10).

"I have loved you with an everlasting love; I have drawn you with loving-kindness" (Jeremiah 31:3).

ENCOUNTER

God's main trait is love. And love is the greatest of the fruits given by the Holy Spirit. The command to love fulfills the Ten Commandments and the entire law. "The goal of this command is love, which comes from a pure heart and a good conscience and a sincere faith" (1 Timothy 1:5).

We're to love the Lord our God with "all our heart, soul, mind, and strength" (Matthew 22:37, Mark 12:28). "Though you have not seen him, you love him" (1 Peter 1:8). Peter did see Jesus and did love Him. Today though we can't see Jesus, we know He's present and we grow to love Him.

We're born into a physical body and live in a fallen sinful state. Yet God loves each of us. He loves you as if you're the only person alive. God hates sin, but He loves people. He sent His Son to die for us. "But God demonstrates his own love for us in this: While we were still sinners, Christ died for us" (Romans 5:8).

I heard of a woman who felt so low she had tattooed on her body the label "Unloved." God loves the unloved, the ugly, the low, the persecuted, the poor, the widow(er), the adulterer, the immigrant, the weak, the sick, the hungry, the addict, the prostitute, the alcoholic, the homeless, the wounded, the abuser, the abused, the condemned, the ill, the impaired, the prisoner, the liar, the murderer, the thief, the tormented, and the sinner.

". . . It is not the healthy who need a doctor, but the sick. I have not come to call the righteous, but sinners" (Mark 2:17). Don't wait to receive your cure from the Great Physician.

The attributes of love, listed in 1 Corinthians 13:4-8, are God's characteristics. Love is patient and kind. Love doesn't envy or boast; love is not proud. Love is not rude or self-seeking or easily angered. Love keeps no record of wrongs. Love doesn't delight in evil but rejoices with the truth. Love always protects, trusts, hopes, and perseveres. Love never fails.

Romans 8:35 asks, "Who shall separate us from the love of Christ?" No one shall! ". . . Neither death nor life, neither angels nor demons, neither the present nor the future, nor any powers, neither height nor depth, nor anything else in all creation, will be able to separate us from the love of God that is in Christ Jesus our Lord" (Romans 8:38, 39).

PRAY: *"Lord, teach me love. Teach me of You."*

BEFORE OUR JOURNEY ENDS

Our spiritual journey began with creation. We end with rebirth through God's gift of salvation, the starting point of Eternal Life. "And this is what he promised us— even eternal life" (1 John 2:25).

We're each accountable for our actions and for our eternity. But know that religion alone cannot save you without spiritual rebirth.

Religion is man trying to make himself right with God. Christianity is Jesus already having laid the foundation to make you right with God. Christianity is God finding you, approaching you, and telling you that you're good enough if you will turn back to Him, repent, and surrender.

Religion will have men worship such idols as minerals, foods, plants, animals, spirits, the sun, fire, or other men. Religion is about what man tries to do to reform to make himself holy! Growing your hair or shaving it, head coverings, facial or body markings, piercings, cuttings, blood-lettings, pilgrimages, sanctified garments, water rites, righteous deeds, abstinence, self-denial, doing good, church attendance, penance, scourgings, fasting, starvation, showy prayers, traditions, holding church office, and giving gifts to the gods are all evidence of some religion.

These "good works" are for men, not for God, and they will never change your heart. Your excellent deeds cannot and will not lessen or erase your sin. Goodness through self-effort isn't acceptable to God. ". . . All our righteous acts are like filthy rags" (Isaiah 64:6). ". . . No one living is righteous before you" (Psalm 143:2).

Perhaps you've attended a church, synagogue, or temple for many years. You may even have held a high position there, but you've never experienced the second birth. Becoming spiritually reborn is the most important life event for you that God offers on earth.

When you stand before God, what will be your defense for your life? Do you want Jesus to step forth, tell the Father that He paid for your sins, and then have Him lead you into heaven? ". . . God will redeem my life from the grave; he will surely take me to himself" (Psalm 49:15).

You don't have to work your way to heaven. If you've been hoping to squeeze in as a reward for your goodness, sorry, you can't earn heaven. No retribution is required, no reparation, no payment. That's man's way! Works won't get you there, no matter how good you are, have been, will be, or hope to be.

Jesus rose from the dead and He's seated at God's right hand. ". . . Christ died for our sins according to the Scriptures, that he was buried, that he was raised on the third day according to the Scriptures" (1 Corinthians 15:3, 4).

"Now this is eternal life: that they may know you, the only true God, and Jesus Christ, whom you have sent" (John 17:3).

Your heart is important in this encounter. It's one thing to acknowledge that Jesus existed in history, but it's quite another to accept Him to be your salvation. Turn to Him. Jesus is the way; He's your only hope. Pray now to Jesus and if heaven doesn't open up to you, prove me wrong.

PRAY: *"I don't fully understand everything that I've read here, but I want to abandon myself to You. I recognize that I'm in need of You, Jesus, to be my Savior. I can't survive this life by myself any longer. I've tried to become holy in Your sight, but there's not enough I can do. Jesus, change me, help me. Forgive my sins. I'm weak. Come into my heart. I surrender, Lord. Save me."*

If you prayed this prayer from your heart, and meant it, then you very likely just entered God's Kingdom through the door of His Son, Jesus Christ. If you did, you will know it. Be happy for ". . . there is rejoicing in the presence of the angels of God over one sinner who repents" (Luke 15:10).

Great promises are now yours. You're a new person. ". . . If anyone is in Christ, he is a new creation; the old has gone, the new has come!" (2 Corinthians 5:17). Your sins are forgiven and forgotten. "God made you alive with Christ. He forgave us all our sins, having canceled the written code, with its regulations, that was against us and that stood opposed to us; he took it away, nailing it to the cross" (Colossians 2:13,14). You have a divine helper. "Never will I leave you; never will I forsake you" (Hebrews 13:5). You have a new home. ". . . Our citizenship is in heaven" (Ephesians 3:20).

God's commitment to you is Eternal life. Let Him depose you as the false master of your destiny. Let Him be your Lord and King.

If you have a personal relationship with your Creator, speak to Him through the prayers of your lips and heart. And let Him speak to you through reading your Bible and by His leading through His Spirit who now lives in you.

Once you have experienced the second birth, or even if you're still searching (or aren't sure), find a church with Bibles in the pews, where the Scriptures are taught, and where you're encouraged to get your own Bible and read it.

Which denomination is best? Jesus said, "He who is not with me is against me . . ." (Luke 11:23). The "true church" is all Christians, collectively, who have a personal relationship with Christ, regardless of the denomination they attend. The early church, for example, met in homes. What's most important is your relationship with God through Christ. Yet, being part of a Christian community is helpful. "Let us not give up meeting together, as some are in the habit of doing, but let us encourage one another— and all the more as you see the Day approaching" (Hebrews 10:25). That means attending a local church or home meeting with people of like faith.

A new Christian is vulnerable, like a newborn. Please be wary of any church, no matter how sincere the attendees or how happy they appear, that imposes cultlike restrictions on you, and whose purposes may be to exploit you.

And make sure to tell someone else what happened to you. "That if you confess with your mouth, 'Jesus is Lord,' and believe in your heart that God raised him from the dead, you will be saved" (Romans 10:9).

Be Christ's witness. "But you will receive power when the Holy Spirit comes on you; and you will be my witnesses in Jerusalem, and in all Judea and Samaria, and to the ends of the earth" (Acts 1:8). Put another way, speak out! "I am not ashamed of the gospel, because it is the power of God for the salvation of everyone who believes: first for the Jew, then for the Gentile. For in the gospel a righteousness from God is revealed, a righteousness that is by faith from first to last, just as it is written: 'The righteous will live by faith'" (Romans 1:16, 17).

If you took this journey, I believe that you were transformed or changed somehow. If you didn't encounter God, perhaps you're holding back. It's hard to accept truth, especially if it's different from anything you've ever imagined. And it's never easy to reverse your life, for belief in Jesus may require you to pay a price of harsh personal consequences.

Examine yourself firmly, because this is important. Perhaps you don't want to decide, though you know you must. You may not want to be held responsible, but you're accountable whether you decide or not.

His voice is calling you. ". . . He is our God and we are the people of his pasture, the flock under his care. Today, if you hear his voice, do not harden your heart(s) . . ." (Psalm 95:7, 8).

Please take hold of this promise now and come into the light. "For God so loved the world that he gave his one and only Son, that whoever believes in him shall not perish but have eternal life. For God did not send his Son into the world to condemn the world, but to save the world through him. Whoever believes in him is not condemned, but whoever does not believe stands condemned already because he has not believed in the name of God's one and only Son. This is the verdict: Light has come into the world, but men loved darkness instead of light because their deeds were evil. Everyone who does evil hates the light, and will not come into the light for fear that his deeds will be exposed. But whoever lives by the truth comes into the light, so that it may be seen plainly that what he has done has been done through God" (John 3:16 – 21).

Finally, I must be blunt. Your only hope is God, through God's Son, Jesus. I don't know about those who were born before Jesus Christ . . . I don't know about those who live in isolated areas and have never heard of Jesus Christ. I only know about me and about the reader of this book. All the answers you need are in the Holy Bible. Jesus is the premise upon which I place my own future. Take Him for now and for the Eternal Life to come.

Find Eternal Life. Embrace eternity with both arms. Tie it down with all your heart, mind, soul, and strength. God will never let you go!

"Now this is eternal life: that they may know you, the only true God, and Jesus Christ, whom you have sent" (John 17:3).

APPENDIX: WHEN WILL MESSIAH COME?

A wonder of history—and significant evidence of God's existence—occurred in 1948 when Israel became a nation. A scattered people came together after nearly two thousand years. Earlier I cited Amos 9:14, 15 and Ezekiel 38:8, two predictions of modern Israel. Also, Jesus hinted at the regathering of Israel in His "Olivet Discourse." In Matthew 24:20 He foresaw the days we live in and the tribulation to come saying, "Pray that your flight will not take place in winter or on the Sabbath." In order to have a Sabbath in Israel there must be Jewish people living in Israel at the time of the end. The modern relocation of the Jewish people to their homeland has been fiery since its inception.

In 1948 many Palestinians living in Israel fled, warned by Arab nations that they were about to attack and destroy Israel. Again, in June 1967, Israel had to save itself. Its neighbors Egypt, Syria, and Jordan set up a naval blockade and massed their armed forces on Israel's borders. Israel countered with a preemptive strike against the three nations in what has been called the Six-Day War.

Following the brief war, Israel claimed Jerusalem, the West Bank region, Golan Heights, Sinai Desert, and Gaza Strip. After the defeat, eight Arab heads of state convened an emergency summit in Khartoum, The Sudan, to eliminate Israeli "aggression."

The meeting ended in September 1967 with the Khartoum Resolutions. Arab leaders committed to these main principles: "No peace with Israel, no recognition of Israel, no negotiations with it, and insistence on the rights of the Palestinian people in their own country." The first three principles effectively established the climate for what would become organized Middle East terrorism.

Within a year of the summit, airplane hijackings, airport bombings, commercial airline bombings, and assorted other bombings by terrorists became the norm throughout the world. Prior to the summit, terrorist homicides of innocent civilians outside Israel were virtually nonexistent.

You'd be right to think that Middle Eastern politics should probably be the theme of another book. However, the Bible predicts that the reestablishment of Israel and accompanying strife will occur in the end times right before the return of Jesus Christ. And Jesus' deity is a major theme of this work.

Jesus predicted Israel's regathering from the nations, as symbolized by the fig tree. "Now learn this lesson from the fig tree: As soon as its twigs get tender and its leaves come out, you know that summer is near. Even so, when you see all these things, you know that it is near, right at the door. I tell you the truth, this generation will certainly not pass away until all these things have happened" (Matthew 24:32-34). Israel has blossomed. Is Jesus at the door?

It's no coincidence that there's war in the Middle East and that Israel occupies center stage of the world theater. The turmoil is not likely to go away, except for a brief period of three and a half years before the return of Jesus Christ, who will finally bring world peace.

These major events, yet to come as of this writing, are predicted in the Bible:

<u>The Seventieth "Week" of Daniel</u>. The Old Covenant prophet Daniel made a prediction of seventy very significant weeks. The first sixty-nine weeks would each follow the other. But the final, or seventieth, week would be separated from the first sixty-nine weeks by hundreds of years.

The first sixty-nine weeks of Daniel ended with the crucifixion of Jesus. Please see DAY 16, DAYBREAK, for more on Daniel's sixty-nine weeks. Daniel's seventieth week, described in Daniel 9:24 and Daniel 9:27, hasn't occurred yet. That "week" is actually a seven-year period, called a *shabua* in Hebrew.

The final seven-year period of Daniel's weeks, Daniel's seventieth week, is known in Christianity as the Tribulation. The seven-year period is generally split into two equal periods of three and a half years. The Tribulation will see many significant events. The Hebrew temple in Jerusalem will be rebuilt. A false messiah, called the antichrist or beast, will attain world power.

The antichrist will bring three and a half years of world peace. The peace will be followed by three and a half years of major war unlike any known before, called the Great Tribulation. After the seven year Tribulation, Jesus Christ will return as the victorious Savior, Messiah ben David, for whom many Jewish people have waited. He will usher in world peace and salvation.

This illustration may help to visualize Daniel's seventy weeks.

Past Events				**Future Events**		
Start <u>Point</u>. 20th year of Arta-xerxes	**<u>Daniel's 69 Weeks</u>**	**End <u>Point</u>. Jesus' Death**	**2nd Temple razed**	**Hundreds of years elapsed until the 3rd Temple will be built**	**<u>Daniel's 70th Week</u>. 7 Year Tribulation. 3rd Temple built. Antichrist.**	**Return of Messiah Jesus**
B.C. 445	- 476 years -	A.D. 31	A.D. 70	A.D. 1945, 1948, 1967, 1973, 1993, 2???	-3.5 years| 3.5 years- of world |"Great peace |Tribulation"	

Jesus claimed to be the Jewish Messiah as this brief dialogue with Pontius Pilate shows. "'Are you the king of the Jews?' asked Pilate. 'Yes, it is as you say,' Jesus replied" (Mark 15:2). Many Jewish people do not recognize Jesus as their Messiah because He did not institute political victory before He died. Yet, the Bible shows us two views, advents or comings, of the Messiah:

The first view is, the suffering Savior, who brought spiritual victory over sin and death. Jesus, or Messiah ben (son of) Joseph, was Jesus at His first visit. The prophet Zechariah predicted that the Messiah would come humbly. "Rejoice greatly, O Daughter of Zion! Shout, Daughter of Jerusalem! See, your king comes to you, righteous and having salvation, gentle and riding on a donkey, on a colt, the foal of a donkey" (Zechariah 9:9). Jesus entered Jerusalem on a colt and a donkey in fulfillment of Zechariah's prophecy. (See Matthew 21:1-9.) Jesus was crucified in A.D. 31.

The second view is the victorious Savior, Messiah ben (son of) David, the victorious Jesus at His Second coming, to be seen by all the earth. Jesus will return as victor, described in Revelation 1:7, following the completion of the seven-year Tribulation.

<u>The Hebrew temple</u>. Rabbinic Judaism, that is widely practiced today, has replaced sacrifice with repentance and good deeds. But good works cannot fulfill God's stringent requirements for goodness. The Bible says that the third temple will be rebuilt in Jerusalem, presumably on the ancient temple mount called Mount Moriah. The "Holy of Holies," the place for animal sacrifice will be restored. The first temple was destroyed by Babylon and the second was destroyed in A. D. 70 by ancient Rome.

The major issue preventing the building of the third temple is that the Temple Mount where the first two Temples stood, is now one of Islam's holy sites. In 1967, Israeli Minister of Defense Moshe Dayan, even after occupying Jerusalem, authorized the Moslem Wakf to continue to rule the mount. The Temple Mount is the third holiest site for Islam after the Kaaba in Mecca and the Prophet's Mosque in Medina, both in Arabia. Since 1967 Jewish people pray at a wall below the Temple Mount called the Western Wall, though the wall was never a wall of the Temple. And Jewish people, for the most part, have not been permitted access to the Temple Mount. Even so, no wall of the second temple remains on the mount.

The mosque known as the Dome of the Rock has occupied space on the Temple Mount beginning with the plans for its construction in A. D. 685. It would be irresponsible conjecture to guess what will happen, if anything, to that mosque. Yet, the Bible is clear that the Hebrew temple will be rebuilt. There are three sites on the Temple Mount that have been proposed to be where the original Temple stood. The primary spot is where the Dome of the Rock stands. There's another potential place to the North of the Dome of the Rock and a third to the South.

A major obstacle in rebuilding the temple is to know exactly where to build it, where to place the foundation. Without access to the Temple Mount the task is virtually impossible. Another obstacle is that in order to rebuild the temple, the builders might inadvertently tread on the site of the Holy of Holies and desecrate the spot.

Each year Jewish people celebrate the festival of Chanukah. That holiday celebrates the purification and rededication of the holy temple. There are organizations in Israel today preparing to rebuild the third temple. They are gathering resources, material like holy vessels, and people, to build the temple and reinstitute temple sacrifice.

<u>The Man of Peace.</u> The Bible describes how at the time the temple is rebuilt, a world leader will rise and offer world peace. And, oh, how the world needs peace! The Bible calls this person the antichrist. He will bring temporary peace, three and a half years of world peace, either a global treaty or perhaps one world religion. Ultimately, he'll want to be worshipped as God.

Paul says of the beast, "He will oppose and will exalt himself over everything that is called God or is worshiped, so that he sets himself up in God's temple, proclaiming himself to be God" (2 Thessalonians 2:4).

Jesus said, ". . . When you see standing in the holy place 'the abomination that causes desolation,' spoken of through the prophet Daniel—let the reader understand— then let those who are in Judea flee to the mountains" (Matthew 24:15, 16). The abomination, or the beast, cannot stand in the holy place, unless there is a holy place. That is, unless the temple is rebuilt. We do know that the Bible predicts the Temple will be rebuilt before Messiah comes.

The antichrist, the unholy beast, will deceive the world and will stand in the Holy Place in the rebuilt temple, three and a half years from the start of the Tribulation, as Matthew 24:15 predicts. "And he performed great and miraculous signs, even causing fire to come down from heaven to earth in full view of men . . . he deceived the inhabitants of the earth . . ." (Revelation 13:13, 14).

The abominable person will erect an idol in the temple. ". . . He ordered them to set up an image in honor of the beast . . . He was given power to give breath to the image of the first beast" (Revelation 13:14, 15).

"He will confirm a covenant with many for one 'seven.' . . ." (Daniel 9:27).

"The coming of the lawless one will be in accordance with the work of Satan displayed in all kinds of counterfeit miracles, signs and wonders, and in every sort of evil that deceives those who are perishing. They perish because they refused to love the truth and so be saved" (2 Thessalonians 2:9, 10).

<u>The Great Tribulation.</u> World peace will end after three and a half years (also called the 1260 days in Revelation 11:3) and then the Great Tribulation will begin. The second half of those

seven years will be a time of unparalleled anguish that will come upon the earth, destruction unlike any known before.

". . . In the middle of the 'seven' [after 3 1/2 years] he will put an end to sacrifice and offering" (Daniel 9:27). The beast will cause the sacrifice in the rebuilt Temple to cease. "From the time that the daily sacrifice is abolished and the abomination that causes desolation is set up, there will be 1,290 days [or 3 1/2 years]" (Daniel 12:11).

Jerusalem surrounded by enemies. "I am going to make Jerusalem a cup that sends all the surrounding peoples reeling. Judah will be besieged as well as Jerusalem" (Zechariah 12:2). Hasn't this been the state of the world since 1948, the inception of Israel? And hasn't the focus of world peace been centered on the Middle East conflict?

Even so, we are admonished to pray for Israel. God will bless the nation that comes to Israel's aid. "Pray for the peace of Jerusalem: 'May those who love you be secure'" (Psalm 122:6).

Ezekiel 38. Ezekiel predicts great battles, when Israel will be attacked. Daniel, in Daniel 11:40, speaks of an attack on Israel by the kingdoms of the North and the South. Ezekiel names some of these nations as far south as Africa and as far north as eastern Europe and Russia.

When the wars and the Great Tribulation become so oppressive, at the climax of world destruction, Messiah will intervene. Jesus predicted, "For then there will be great distress, unequaled from the beginning of the world until now—and never to be equaled again. If those days had not been cut short, no one would survive, but for the sake of the elect those days will be shortened" (Matthew 24:21, 22).

The return of the Messiah. "I saw heaven standing open . . . His eyes are like blazing fire . . . He is dressed in a robe dipped in blood, and his name is the Word of God. The armies of heaven were following him, riding on white horses and dressed in fine linen, white and clean" (Revelation 19:11-14).

There will be signs in the heavens before He returns. "Immediately after the distress of those days 'the sun will be darkened, and the moon will not give its light; the stars will fall from the sky, and the heavenly bodies will be shaken.'" (Matthew 24:29).

He will be visible, bodily, in the eastern sky and coming upon the clouds. "For as lightning that comes from the east is visible even in the west, so will be the coming of the Son of Man" (Matthew 24:27).

"At that time the sign of the Son of Man will appear in the sky, and all the nations of the earth will mourn. They will see the Son of Man coming on the clouds of the sky, with power and great glory" (Matthew 24:30).

"In the future you will see the Son of Man sitting at the right hand of the Mighty One and coming on the clouds of heaven" (Matthew 26:64).

"In my vision at night I looked, and there before me was one like a son of man, coming with the clouds of heaven" (Daniel 7:13)

When Christ ascended to heaven, an angel predicted that He would return from the sky. ". . . This same Jesus, who has been taken from you into heaven, will come back in the same way you have seen him go into heaven" (Acts 1:11).

Ezekiel predicted that Messiah will return to the Mount of Olives. He will reenter Jerusalem through the East Gate (now walled up) as He did on the first Palm Sunday and enter the rebuilt temple. "The glory of the LORD entered the temple through the gate facing east" (Ezekiel 43:4). ". . . The glory of the God of Israel coming from the east. His voice was like the roar of rushing waters, and the land was radiant with his glory" (Ezekiel 43:2, emphasis mine).

"His feet were like bronze glowing in a furnace, and his voice was like the sound of rushing waters" (Revelation 1:15, emphasis mine).

When Jesus brings peace, the world will finally be at political peace. May you, the reader, also find spiritual peace through Jesus Christ, the Prince of Peace.

"For to us a child is born, to us a son is given, and the government will be on his shoulders. And he will be called Wonderful Counselor, Mighty God, Everlasting Father, Prince of Peace" (Isaiah 9:6).

(Note: Some of the Scriptures used in this Appendix may also be found in Hal Lindsey's book, The Late Great Planet Earth. [21])

INDEX BY TOPIC

BIBLIOGRAPHY

(Endnotes)

[1] Robert Jastrow, God and the Astronomers, (New York: Reader's Library, W. W. Norton & Co., 1978) 116.

[2] "Adam's Genes," Time Magazine, June 5, 1995: 21.

[3] Stanley Rosenthal, One God or Three?, (West Collingswood: The Spearhead Press, 1978)

[4] F. Kenton Beshore,The Messiah of the Targums, Talmuds, and Rabbinical Writers, (Los Angeles: World Bible Society, 1971) Chart 10

[5] Eusebius, The Ecclesiastical History of Eusebius Pamphilus, (Grand Rapids: Baker Book House, 1993) 44, Book I-Chapter 13.

[6] F. Kenton Beshore,The Messiah of the Targums, Talmuds, and Rabbinical Writers, (Los Angeles: World Bible Society, 1971) Chart 27

[7] Frank Stockton, The Lady, or the Tiger? and Other Stories, (New York, Scribner, 1914)

[8] Fyodor Dostoevsky, The Brothers Karamazov, (New York, Alfred A. Knopf, Inc., 1990) 249, 250.

[9] Ibid., 260.

[10] Frank Morison, Who Moved the Stone, (Grand Rapids, MI: Zondervan, 1987)

[11] Josh McDowell, More Than a Carpenter, (Wheaton, Illinois: Living Books, 1989) 89-99.

[12] Flavius Josephus, "Antiquities of the Jews," Josephus Complete Works, (Grand Rapids: Kregel Publications, 1978) 379, Book 18-Chapter three-Verse three.

[13] Alfred, Lord Tennyson,"Crossing The Bar," Immortal Poems of the English Language, ed. Oscar Williams, (New York: Washington Square Press, 1969) 397.

[14] C. S. Lewis, Mere Christianity, (New York: Scribner, 1952) 167.

[15] Emmet Fox, Sermon on the Mount, (New York: Harper & Row, 1935) Preface.

[16] F. Kenton Beshore,The Messiah of the Targums, Talmuds, and Rabbinical Writers, (Los Angeles: World Bible Society, 1971) Chart 25

[17] Mary Shelley, Frankenstein, or the Modern Prometheus, (New York: Bantam Books, 1991) 37, 39.

[18] William T. Ellis, Billy Sunday The Man and His Message, (Chicago: Moody Press, 1959) 183.

[19] Charles Dickens, A Tale of Two Cities, (New York: Signet Classics, The New American Library of World Literature, 1964) 347.

[20] Ibid., 365.

[21] Hal Lindsey, The Late Great Planet Earth, (New York: Bantam Books, 1970).

About the Author

Dennis Kaufman was born in the Bronx, New York, graduated from Villanova University, and studied Old Testament at Alliance Theological Seminary. He works as an Information Technology consultant. Dennis completed two screenplays and is writing a novel about rebuilding the Hebrew Temple in Jerusalem. He was published in *Catholic Digest, The Evangelical Beacon,* and the *Victims of Pan Am 103* website. Dennis once accompanied a narcotics officer for an inner city story. With roots in Judaism and Catholicism, Dennis became spiritually awakened in 1980, when he believed in Jesus as his Messiah. He and his wife, Fernanda, have a son and three daughters; they attend Montvale Evangelical Free Church, New Jersey where he's been an Elder and Sunday school teacher. Author may be contacted at "EASTGATEDEV@yahoo.com"

Made in the USA
Columbia, SC
27 July 2023

20984076R00064